Loving My Actual Life

AN EXPERIMENT IN RELISHING WHAT'S RIGHT IN FRONT OF ME

ALEXANDRA KUYKENDALL

BakerBooks

a division of Baker Publishing Group
Grand Rapids, Michigan

Published by Baker Books
a division of Baker Publishing Group
P.O. Box 6287, Grand Rapids, MI 49516-6287
www.bakerbooks.com

Printed in the United States of America

Library of Congress Cataloging-in-Publication Data
Names: Kuykendall, Alexandra, author.
Title: Loving my actual life : an experiment in relishing what's right in front of me / Alexandra Kuykendall.
Description: Grand Rapids : Baker Books, 2016. | Includes bibliographical references.
Identifiers: LCCN 2015049580 | ISBN 9780801007811 (pbk.)
Subjects: LCSH: Christian women—Religious life.
Classification: LCC BV4527 .K854 2016 | DDC 248.8/43—dc23
LC record available at http://lccn.loc.gov/2015049580

16   17   18   19   20   21   22   7   6   5   4

For my main cast of characters.

Derek, Gabi, Genevieve, Gracelynn, and Giulianna,
I thank God you are the people in my actual life.

Contents

Preface

A LETTER TO YOU

Hi, Friend,

We likely haven't met in real life, but I consider you a friend for a few reasons. First, you're ready to hear my experiences as I journey on a nine-month experiment to appreciate and cherish my life. My actual life. With all its quirks, frustrations, disappointments, surprises, and gifts. This is what friends do, sit and listen and cheer each other on. So thank you for being a willing listener.

And second, I suspect you've picked up this book because we are somewhat kindred spirits, friends in the journey of life. We are both facing days of incredible speed and desiring something different because this pace just doesn't feel right. We know with certainty that we must be made for more than merely tolerating our circumstances; we want to know how to thrive within them. Especially if we don't have a lot of opportunity to change the major things. We want to love *this* life today.

I must also recognize what I don't know about you. I don't know your financial or marital status. Whether you have children, an extended family, or a close circle of friends.

Your emotional or spiritual health. Your age. Your education. Your work, paid or unpaid. Those details all matter because they impact *your* actual life. They shape you, inform you, and influence you as you make thousands of daily decisions.

I find most people are working hard to live life "right." Whatever our right might be. And then real life gets in the way. Singleness or infertility or underemployment or whiny children may not be what we expected, or hoped for, but here we are. We all have our ideal and then we also all have our reality. They rarely match up. This is a book about savoring the reality.

The last few years I've been following my friend and mentor Karen's advice. "Do what only *you* can do," she told me during my fourth pregnancy as I struggled with work-family decisions. She emphasized *you*. I was the only one who could be Derek's wife and my girls' mother. Other responsibilities could be shared, even totally discarded on my part. It helped me say no to some obligations as I realized there were many things I *could* do, but didn't *need* to do. But even with that intentional decision-making matrix, I sensed I was still not living my best life. I needed a fresh start. And that is where the experiment was born.

In this experiment we're going to hang out in the element that *is*. Not what we could be, should be, or wish were true about our lives, but what actually *is*. To find a contentment that doesn't merely resign itself to circumstances we wish were different, but appreciates the daily routine we're in right now. Because God gave us each one unique life. Meant to be lived out in our *actual* situations. I don't want the gifts he's offered to go unnoticed nor the opportunities wasted. I want to live into where he's called me and me alone.

Looking at life from a global perspective, through the eyes of someone whose physical needs aren't being met, I recognize that I am living a pretty comfortable, even charmed, life. I don't want this experiment to simply be a list of first world pains. But the truth is my reality *is* embedded in the first world and there are barriers preventing me from appreciating God's gifts right around me. I want to identify and overcome these barriers so I can truly relish the goodness that surrounds me.

You'll be reading along as I stumble through the experiment and discover what helps me in the relishing. Some findings surprise me and change how I approach my days. At the end of each month I share what I've learned and the practices I'll most likely continue in my daily rhythms. You'll also find some questions to get you thinking about how you are doing in the given area of your own life. And a verse or two from the Bible that you can meditate on or even memorize as you consider God's unchanging nature and desire in the midst of your "crazy busy."

My process is not always pretty or neat. But truly my hope is that my stumblings will stir questions in you about what it means to love your actual, unique life. That it might be an impetus for you to consider the question, "What if my fresh start started right here?"

I'll close this letter with an invitation for you to join me, maybe even with your actual friends, in this experiment of relishing the goodness that is here and present. Consider the questions at the end of each chapter, do your own version of the experiment for a month, a week, or a day at a time, to discover what works in helping you love your actual life.

Your friend in the experiment,
Alex

Introduction
THE RECALIBRATING OF MY DAYS

The Need

The alarm on my phone sounds. As my hand searches the top of my hamper for the source of the church bell chimes alarm, my thoughts are already at yesterday's unfinished to-do list. Despite the prior day's frenzied efforts, I hadn't checked everything off the list and had fallen into bed with part of me feeling as though I'd failed. I awake to a lingering feeling of urgency from unfinished work. As I swing my feet to the floor, I feel my jaw tighten and my heart rate speed up. Back to yesterday's crazy-busy speed in a matter of seconds.

And now the whirlwind of the day: the waking of children, feeding them, throwing clothes (any clothes!) on their bodies, having an argument (or three) about them making their lunches, dropping them off at various schools, clicking in and out of car seats a thousand times, bringing not-yet-in-school children home, putting them in front of the television while I try unsuccessfully to get just a little work done, counting down the hours until I need to begin the school pick-ups, throwing two loads of laundry through the cycles so they can move from the dirty pile to the equally huge clean pile in our laundry room, getting the littles (as we call the two youngest in our house) back into the car, school pick-ups for the bigs (you guessed it, the older two), realizing we have nothing for dinner, scouring cupboards for something that will qualify (because it's too late in the day to consider freezer options), waiting in my minivan in the driveway for my husband to pull in so I can pull out and head to soccer practice with one of my older girls, yelling some type of dinner instructions at him over my shoulder as I peel out, trying to cram another hour of work in during soccer practice, coming home, eating, putting girls to bed, checking emails one more time, and collapsing, knowing tomorrow will hold another, almost identical agenda and pace.

A typical day in the recent span of my life, and it is where this story begins.

I was living day after day crammed full with no foreseeable end to the crazy-making. Ever. With a three-year-old as our caboose child, it could be roughly fifteen more years of this kind of crazy-making. I was operating in perma-exhaustion, which, I'm sure you can imagine, made me a sweet and lovely person.

When I started speaking to people in bullet points rather than complete sentences to maximize efficiency, I knew I wasn't living as I should. And yet when I considered all the elements of my life, all the things that took up time and attention, I recognized they were *all* good things. My family, for sure. My work offered me an outlet and greater purpose, not to mention income. My church kept me grounded. My friends offered sanity. My kids' activities were limited because, believe it or not, I truly was trying to have some semblance of control over our family schedule. On their own, all good things, but compounded they became more than 24-hours' worth of commitments. It was simply impossible for one woman to do all the things I was attempting. I was not living a sustainable life.

This whirlwind of an existence collided with a catalyst. A life event that grabbed my attention and told me my time to fully live is now: I toured middle schools. That's right, my eldest daughter was leaving the childhood years of elementary school, where everything felt safe and the future felt long, to start middle school, and that triggered something in me. Part nostalgia, part fear, part panic that I would wake up the next day and she'd be fully grown and gone. I knew I needed to be paying better attention to today.

And then Derek came home from work and reported a conversation he'd had with a man a few years ahead of us in parenting (those kinds of conversations are either hopeful or horrifying). This is what that man said: "From zero to eleven the years are long, from eleven on they fly." Derek and I looked at each other and knew we were headed toward free fall.

Something drastic was in order. A recalibrating of my days. Of my time. So I could appreciate this one life that I've been given. (Oh yeah, and I turned forty this year too, which means

> *I needed a reordering, a restart, a recalibration of my days.*

I'm due for a midlife crisis of sorts.) And when I looked around at my friends as we sped by each other in the school pick-up line, I felt I was not alone in this plate-spinning life.

My friends Rob and Erica just took a year off and moved their family of five to Argentina for twelve months. I watched on Facebook as they tried new foods, made new friends, and took adventures that felt daring and reminiscent of my globetrotting childhood. And yet I knew that wasn't the type of drastic move that would be a reality, or really even a desire, for our family. *There must be a way to create a fresh start right here*, I thought. To love the life I actually have and not one I fantasize about because it's an escape from my reality. Could I make small tweaks to be more present?

But how does one fully savor the right here when there seem to be barriers in the way? The "if onlys" and the "whens." If only I had more money or more time, I could . . . When I have this in place, then . . . I couldn't wait for the perfect life to arrive to enjoy it. I could wish my current circumstances away for days on end, but the major things were unlikely to change. I needed to work with what I had right in front of me. I needed to learn to love my actual life.

I needed a reordering, a restart, a recalibration of my days.

The Experiment

Once I decided a change was in order, I looked for the prescriptive formula for loving my actual life. Online, in books, talking with friends. But not for long, because I knew if there was a universal, magic way to make all this happen, everyone would be talking about it. The only glaring finding was that different approaches work for different people. There had to be that mix that was just mine, that would look different from my friend's or my sister-in-law's. I needed to do an experiment that would help me figure out how to better manage *my* actual life. An experiment, because trial and error were sure to be involved. My days would be the laboratory. What I did needed to be different from the way I'd been doing things up to this point, and it needed to be tailored to *my* circumstances. My aim was the right here, the right now. I was not working toward some long-term goal; I wanted to relish the immediate. Today.

But what could I change? Leaving my family wasn't an option; they were here to stay and so was I. My marriage needed more attention, not less, if we were going to be anything more than carpool partners. I'd sorely neglected some friendships because I was just "too busy" to spend time with people. It all sounds rather pathetic, doesn't it? All that meant the big item on my daily schedule that could be reworked was work.

So I did what any sane woman would do—I quit my part-time job. Okay, that sounds more drastic than it actually was. But I did significantly shift things around at work, including pulling back on my time commitment and moving my employment status to contractor so I could have more control over my schedule and workload. I wanted to be able to drop off my girls at school and pick them up from school. But I also wanted to feed them dinner and offer them clean underwear on a regular basis. (Not to mention I found it a bit ironic that I worked for one of our country's largest mothering organizations and I was exploding at my children at every turn because I was unraveling from stress.) And when I mapped out the years in front of us, with our eldest moving into middle school, I figured out we'd have three girls at three different schools from this point forward. That meant six (yes, six) trips to a school every day (with no school buses involved, just Mom's taxi). For years on end! Confirmation I couldn't continue with the frantic status quo.

I was afraid if I stepped away from some work opportunities, I would be missing out somehow. And that's when it hit me: I was already missing out on my life. I was stretched so thin I wasn't enjoying any part of it. And then God spoke. Okay, I didn't hear a Charlton Heston–like voice, but I did feel that heart nudge I know to be a holy whisper, which said, *We can do better here.* After all, Jesus is the one who says, "Come to me, all you who are weary and burdened, and I will give you rest."[1] I was weary for sure, and it was as if he was saying, *Just stop for a minute and let's reevaluate. And while we do that, why don't you take a load off?*

From what I know of God (both from my past foibles and what it says in the Scriptures), he is in charge of second chances. In fact, it's kind of his specialty. So even though my exhaustion was predominantly self-created, I knew I wasn't a lost cause. I knew he would be gentle with this weary woman. "Now God has us where he wants us, with all the time in this world and the next to shower grace and kindness upon us in Christ Jesus."[2] Yes, I could unabashedly recognize I needed a change and I knew God would be gracious and patient with me in the process.

Derek and I were able to tighten the already tight budget belt to give me more flexibility. But that opening up of the schedule wasn't enough. I could quickly (and we're talking very quickly) begin to fill my freed hours with more commitments that I wasn't that . . . well . . . committed to. I needed to say no to good things that came up to say yes to even better.

So with the schedule as cleared as this working mother of four could make it, I was ready to begin my experiment to love my actual life. I added some intentionality back into my days with one singular focus, one month at a time, for nine months. Each month I chose an area that would feed my heart or make my routines operate more smoothly so I could fully enjoy the gifts I'd been given. I focused on elements I felt were missing altogether or were sorely ignored in my list of priorities. Places where small changes could be made. I alternated my months between more practical areas and more overarching topics that permeated all areas of my life. Whatever the focus, I made it my top priority for the month.

From what I know of God (both from my past foibles and what it says in the Scriptures), he is in charge of second chances. In fact, it's kind of his specialty.

Knowing my own limitations, I looked at each month independent of the others. I simply couldn't make all the changes all the time. Whether it was my morning routine or adding adventure to my day, all negotiable elements of my schedule were planned around making this one area a priority. I wanted to know if these areas of intentionality indeed made a difference. This was an experiment, after all. I couldn't judge their effectiveness in helping me love my actual life unless I truly made the changes in question a priority.

Some months the experiment tended to be more introspective, and in others, more functional. Some elements were more specific to a time of day or task, and others permeated my schedule from morning till night.

And I did this for nine months because I tend to think of life in terms of nine-month blocks. The school calendar never really got out of my system before it began all over again with my own kids starting their "year" in September and ending in May. Fall is my favorite season, in part because I loved the beginning of school and the potential of what could be. And then of course there were babies grown in the darkness, who finally saw the light after nine months. The development of fingernails and internal organs and brain tissue, formed and refined until something beautiful and miraculous came from nothing, at least nothing I could see. It seemed appropriate the experiment would be nine months in length.

Although the experiment was about me, the things I can control and my own satisfaction, other people were involved because my life is intertwined with others. In fact, I have a whole cast of characters. They're varied and imperfect and beautiful. They are my actual people. The ones who laugh and cry with me. Who tell me what I'm good at and not so good at. It's a big cast and impossible to name them all. So I'll give you the lowdown on the main cast of characters: me and the ones I live with.

My Main Cast of Characters

Me: 40 (and fighting it as evidenced by the amount of money spent on coloring my hair)

    Likes: City living, coffee with cream, *Downton Abbey*, thrift store finds, MOPS,[3] Nutella on anything edible, and fall (oh yeah, and cozy sweaters)

    Most likely to be found: Standing in my kitchen

Derek: 40-plus (and rockin' the gray sideburns and halfsie reading glasses)

> **Likes**: Home improvement projects, barbecue, Colorado, *SNL*, basketball, and his job

> **Most likely to be found**: Driving Denver's streets in his truck

Gabi: 12

> **Likes**: Her iPhone, soccer, puppies, Chevron pattern, the color turquoise, basketball, and Chick-fil-A

> **Most likely to be found**: At soccer practice

Genevieve: 9

> **Likes**: Lego Friends, soccer, basketball, swimming, Denver sports teams, Taylor Swift, and Roald Dahl books

> **Most likely to be found**: Reading in the bedroom loft her daddy built for her

Gracelynn: 5

> **Likes**: Makeup phones,* My Little Pony, the color pink, fashion coloring books, and writing her name

> **Most likely to be found**: Playing "moms" with Giulianna

Giulianna (aka Lalo): 3

> **Likes**: Cake pops, snuggling, the color blue, Power Rangers, Sunday school, and her sisters

> **Most likely to be found**: Asleep in her mom and dad's bed

This cast is my motivation to be more intentional. To be more patient, more present, more satisfied. To be a better woman. I love them with fierce intensity and yet I operate out of depletion, which prevents me from being able to appreciate them in the ways I want to and know I can.

---

* For those who may not be familiar: girls' makeup stored in a case that looks like a cell phone. Yes, they are a thing. Usually decorated with lots of rhinestones, sparkles, and sometimes the picture of a Chihuahua. I know.

My fresh start starts right here. I don't need a New Year's resolution or nine months of perfect timing to get it started (because we all know that will *never* happen). I need to start relishing my life today. One intentional moment, day, month at a time.

New neighbors moved in across the street this year. One day they strung a back-and-forth zigzag canopy of lights across their backyard. We have similar lights hanging over our back patio. Because that's what you do when you are expecting good things to happen, for parties and friends and celebrations to take place. A small detail, but one that says expectation for the beautiful that is going to occur. And that is how I see this experiment, setting the stage of expectation to relish what is right here. To discover what is right in front of me in a new light. And like this string of lights made up of one small bulb after another, this experiment is about one small change after another creating a cumulative effect of loving my actual life.

My fresh
start starts
right here.

Questions for Reflection

1. What is motivating you to make a change to love your actual life?
2. What would you like to get out of this experiment?

Words for My Actual Life

Come to me, all you who are weary and burdened, and I will give you rest. (Matt. 11:28)

MONTH 1

Bring It Down

Quiet

See how nature—trees, flowers, grass—grows in silence; see the stars, the moon and the sun, how they
move in silence. . . . We need silence to be able to touch
souls.

—Mother Teresa

The Need

I am a multitasking maniac whose life pace makes NASCAR drivers jealous. The backdrop to all that busyness is constant noise. Both around me and in my head. I don't have space to think. I frequently tell my children to stop talking so I can remember why I walked over to a certain spot in the kitchen. I am at capacity. No, I'm past capacity, and I need to bring the noise level down to hear my own thoughts. To even remember who I am.

I know I will miss the people noise someday, but practically speaking, I make phone calls in my laundry room just so I can hear the person on the other end, and I hide in my basement office for some alone time.

But as I'm trying to create some quiet space, what am I actually doing down there in my mom cave? I'm back on my computer, taking in all kinds of mental noise. Along with the constant audible noise is the virtual clamor that is at minimum a nonstop chatter. Email, Facebook, Twitter, and Instagram. It is, of course, insta-crazy.

To top it off, I am an introvert. I need quiet time to refuel, and I have a life where I am *never* alone (unless you count when I am driving to and from my dentist appointments, then, yes, I am alone twice a year). So purposely creating quiet is essential to my sanity. I've read that noisy surroundings decrease short-term memory[1] and something as small as a cell phone ringing can increase your blood pressure.[2] No wonder things feel off.

I know I have to start the experiment by stopping. It feels a bit counterintuitive to start with a stop, but my natural tendency when I'm overwhelmed is to do more, not less. I need to be more efficient. Get more things done in an hour, in 24 hours, in a week, than I did yesterday or the day before. I'll get up earlier, stay up later, and multitask more resourcefully, whatever it takes to solve this problem. That's what's gotten me into this predicament in the first place; instead of pulling back, I tend to jump in. But perhaps the key before tackling everything with *more* is to stop. And so that is what I'm doing. Stopping the noise to be able to breathe and let my mind rest.

The Experiment

I intentionally add quiet to my days. To achieve this, I focus on two areas: actual quiet and virtual quiet.

My Actual Approach

Add thirty minutes of intentional alone time daily.

Eliminate social media use.

Set Sundays apart for a quieter routine.

DAY 1

Just to simplify things, I've decided to turn my life upside down with this experiment right in the middle of Christmas. Because nothing else is ever going on this time of year. The truth is, it's like any life change: there's never a perfect time. Besides, this experiment is about enjoying my actual life and that is always right now.

And to complicate the timing even more, a few days ago Derek bought me an early Christmas present, a fancy new phone. Three hours at the Apple store on a Saturday during the Christmas shopping season and he came home to me, a mess of a woman because while he was getting schooled on all things "i," I took four children to the mall to look for basketball shoes that cost the equivalent of a down payment on a house.

He handed me the new phone and we promptly started to argue. It was all too much—the noise, the crowds, the salespeople who, bless them, were barely older than the child I was shopping for and unable to explain why the shoes or the phone cost so much!

In the middle of the argument, I held the phone in his direction. "Take it back. If it's going to cause this much conflict, I don't want it." Not a great start to my new fancy phone, nor was it very gracious of me considering the time and money he just spent to put it in that very hand of mine. Within an hour of receiving this gift, I already had the impulse to turn it off.

The truth is, I need my phone with me. Especially when my children aren't. If the school wants to let me know a child is throwing up or a coach needs to tell me practice is rained out and my girl is standing in the downpour, they need to be able to track me down. So I tend to keep my phone within earshot. But what I don't need is the other noise this device constantly offers: Facebook telling me how awesome someone's week in Hawaii is going or the newsfeed offering all kinds of fascinating stories on the latest trends in handbags.

So Gabi moved my social media icons off my main phone screen to minimize temptation (because my oldest child tends to be my tech support). I gave a little shout-out on Facebook and Instagram that I'd be off through the holidays (just in case anyone desperately missed me, because I was sure, or rather hoping, they would) and closed my computer. And my family cheered.

DAY 2

I'm a cheater. That's all there is to it. I wanted to see how many, if any, responses I got to my farewell proclamation online. That's as pathetic as a person can be, I believe. Day 2 and I've already hit bottom in that I've realized I have almost no self-control, and I care too much about what is happening in a virtual world to keep my own self-imposed rules.

And guess what! My heart sank a little because, though a few people wished me a Merry Christmas, no one begged me to keep posting my witty observations of everyday life. Reality bites.

DAY 4

We went to the mall to see Santa. We being the littles (the ones who still believe), along with Nonna and Grandpa (my mom and stepdad), who treated us to lunch. Two girls with party dresses and shoes and hair brushed. The three-year-old even had a red velvet dress trimmed with white fur (her sister wore it as a Mrs. Claus costume for Halloween).

And of course we had a schedule to keep. Because that's how our life works. I needed to pick up big sisters from their schools in a few hours. So when the elf working Santa's village pulled a rope across the path into the entrance and declared, "Santa is going on a milk and cookie break"—the lady elf pointed to the sign that showed the disclaimer that this was indeed allowed—"and he'll be back at two!" my heart stopped.

Because 2:00 was in forty minutes! I quickly assessed the situation: if we saw him at 2:00 we could make it back across town and to our first school pick-up in time. And then I felt the line already forming behind us. We were *not* giving up our prized place of second in line. So I did what the woman in front of me did: I sat down. On the mall floor. And made my own mama-elf declaration. "I guess we'll just have to wait."

Then I felt the urge. To pull out my phone. And begin the perusing. The surfing. The mindless wandering and time wasting. My mom decided this was the perfect time to sneak away to do a Christmas errand. And my girls pressed their noses against Santa's fence and I watched them. And they came and sat next to me on the floor. And we played rock, paper, scissors. They'd get up, run around a bit, come back to home base, and do a few more rounds. The five-year-old trying to remember what beats what, that scissors cut paper, and the three-year-old littlest sister following along, happy to form her chubby hand into a fist and pound away. All the time I was aware of the itching to pull out my phone to fill this space with noise. But I didn't.

There I was, not on my phone, playing with my girls. Recognizing I wasn't going to make the time go any faster by checking the clock on my device every ninety seconds. So Grandpa sat in his wheelchair and closed his eyes. Nonna shopped. And I played and watched and prayed I would always remember two girls standing on their tiptoes, trying to peek into Santa's workshop to catch a glimpse of the magic.

DAY 5

It's Sunday and in our house that usually means church. Not as a rule, but as a practice. We don't go to school or to the office. But that doesn't mean lots of work doesn't happen the rest of the day. It's a time when we often catch up on housework and homework. When emails can still be written and chores done.

There is a tradition in the Christian church to observe Sunday as a day of rest. A mirror of God's rest on the seventh day after he made everything. We call it the Sabbath. And yet so many of my Sundays are crammed full with all the things that wouldn't fit into the six other crammed-full days of the week. The day might feel a bit different because everyone's home, but it's still work.

But not this Sunday. I wanted to add in some quiet. Besides, our church routine was already mixed up because Derek took Genevieve to a soccer event that morning. Because sometimes the rest of the world does things on Sunday mornings and we want to raise our children in the spirit of the Sabbath, not the rule of it.

So I took the other three to church, came home, and worked on Christmas cards all day long. Cutting, addressing, stickering. As the snow fell, the Broncos game played in the background.

Though the sportscasters' voices sounded through our living room, there was a sense of quiet. A "do things you enjoy instead of things you should do" kind of day. Those chores I knew I needed to get done, laundry and grocery shopping, don't feel restful to me. Besides, I knew they would be there tomorrow. I was going to be intentional about letting today be a different kind of day in my week.

> *I was going to be intentional about letting today be a different kind of day in my week.*

As a bonus, I did something I rarely do (mostly because I'm cheap and our family is nice-sized by most standards and eating out more than every once in a while kills our budget). I ordered take-out. As my children's jaws dropped when I announced I was headed to the Mexican restaurant a few blocks from our house to get our dinner, I felt as though I was giving myself a mini-vacation. I think I caught the spirit of the Sabbath.

DAY 7

My constant urge to pick up my phone is showing me that my default during the pauses in my day is to grab for this device. To check email, Facebook, Twitter, Instagram. It doesn't really matter what it is I'm checking, because it's mindless. And every time I look down I'm missing what's right in front of me. Those beautiful faces. But also the mess. By temporarily eliminating that diversion, I'm recognizing I use that "noise" to distract me from things I want to avoid as well. The uncomfortable in many forms.

I can now see I'm bored. I pick up my phone. I have ten minutes and don't want to do the dishes. I check my email for the third time that day. I think of a phone call I should make, but would rather not, and I peruse the virtual headlines. From practical to emotional, I have been unknowingly using virtual noise to avoid loneliness, dissatisfaction, jealousy. And in turn it's simply making me more lonely, dissatisfied, and jealous.

DAY 8

Today I couldn't deny this new self-awareness, something about me is discontent with the moment and I want to escape. And what am I escaping to? Well, the beautifully edited lives of those I know and those I don't. Which of course rarely makes me feel more satisfied with my own circumstances. How can my dirty house compare with a ski vacation? Or a beautifully decorated table all ready for great food and great conversation?

> I'm recognizing I use that "noise" to distract me from things I want to avoid as well.

I realized today I was viewing real-life moments as potential posts or photo ops. Matching Christmas jammies. The annual pageant with three angels and an innkeeper. Decorating a gingerbread house. Because there is apparently something in me that wants to shout, "See! I *am* a good mom! My kids *are* all that! Agree with me! Validate me! 'Like' me!"

My girls are growing up with this as their normal, the eldest about to get her own Instagram account, and I remembered an article I read last summer about a mom who realized her teenage daughter was never getting a break from the social noise. The constant texting, Snapchatting, or whatevering didn't stop on its own. The mom needed to be the one to quiet it for her daughter's emotional sake. Years ago, when I came home from middle school, I could close my front door and not return to that social scene until the next day. I had quiet.

I need this comparison noise to stop as a woman, so how can I expect my children to self-regulate when I'm practically tearing my eyeballs out to not check Facebook?

DAY 12

It's Sunday again and there we were, all six of us, ending our quiet Sabbath watching *60 Minutes*. Doing our part to bring the average age of viewership down a notch. The Broncos game had just ended and we were too relaxed to turn off the TV. We went right into Anderson Cooper with these words: "Our lives are filled with distractions—email, Twitter, texting, we're constantly connected to technology, rarely alone with just our thoughts. Which is probably why there's a growing movement in America to train people to get around the stresses of daily life."[3]

He went on to tell us that the movement sweeping the nation is "mindfulness." As they showed a retreat where Silicon Valley execs turned in their cell phones and devices for a weekend of quiet, my family all turned and looked at me.

"Mom! That's just like you!" Except I'm not at a retreat and I don't make a gazillion dollars a year for being our family executive. But in some ways, it was like me.

Anderson interviewed John Kabat-Zinn, a longtime practitioner of mindfulness, who explained staying present in the moment, or mindful, can start by focusing on the sensation of breathing in and out. As my family and I lay sprawled on our sofas in front of our TV, we watched people eating together, but in silence, so they could fully taste their food, and sitting legs crossed to focus on their breathing so they could fully focus on the space they occupied. It started to feel a little wackadoodle.

Derek's focus shifted from the screen to me, his eyebrows raised. "What do you think?"

"I don't think it's that different from what people have been doing for a long time. It sounds like meditation to me."

DAY 13

I woke up thinking about meditation. Not something I've ever really practiced, but I know Christians have for centuries. So I dug out my *Spiritual Disciplines Handbook* by Adele Calhoun—a book my church gave us a few years ago and I've had good intentions of reading, but you know the whole over-busy life. As I looked through the table of contents, I found "Breath Prayer," a chapter about a simple prayer structure that follows our breathing pattern. We pray a name of God as we inhale and a desire of our heart as we exhale.

> This short repetitive prayer frees you from linear thought and allows you to begin to pray in your body, not just your mind. It is meant to be a lived, breathing rhythm of surrender. And it is a constant reminder of the One in whose presence you stand.[4]

Okay, when put that way it did sound a lot like mindfulness, but with a focus on God. And I was right about people doing it for a long time. Calhoun says the church, especially the Eastern Orthodox arm, has been practicing breath prayer for "millennia" to live out the command to "pray without ceasing."[5]

I tried it. Breathe in. *Lord Jesus.* Breathe out. *Have mercy on me.* There was so much more I wanted to say, so I could check prayer off my to-do list and move on to the next urgent matter. Breathe in. *Lord Jesus.* Breathe out. *Have mercy on me.*

Even my prayers are noisy, rushed, filled with everything I need to say to God in as efficient a way as possible. And I rarely sit in quiet. Sit. Quiet. Breathe in. *Lord Jesus.* Breathe out. *Have mercy on me.*

DAY 15

I had a rare hour alone today, driving to and from a work Christmas party. Drive time is usually multitask time. I either use it to try to connect with one of my older girls if she's sitting in the front seat next to me or I make phone calls. So there I was, two half-hour blocks of time, perfect to check a few calls off my intensifying holiday to-do list. But I stopped myself. The phone stayed in my purse.

I considered a little seasonal music might put me more in the Christmas spirit. The radio stayed off.

Quiet.

I let my thoughts wander. And then I remembered breath prayer. Why not now? Not exactly pure meditation as I drove down the freeway—I couldn't close my eyes—but as I drove, Breathe in. *Emmanuel.* Breathe out. *Be present.*

DAY 16

It was a difficult night at the Kuykendall house. The kind when the chaos of Christmas and all the extras caught up with us. And one girl in particular fell apart at the seams. If you're wondering what that looks like, it involves screaming and crying. It was an exhaustion-induced meltdown. They happen to the best of us. And as a mom, I wanted to pet her hair and help her fall asleep.

So that's what I did. A bit of snuggling in my bed with a girl wrapped in my arms. And as I tried to create space and quiet for my daughter who desperately needed them, I remembered something I'd read that day in Adele's book: you can teach breath prayer to children to take with them to school as a tool to remember and experience God's presence. Instead of walking her through the prayer, I prayed it for her. Silently, no sound coming out of my mouth, but fully audible to the One who hears our prayers. Inhale. *Lord Jesus.* Exhale. *Have mercy on her.* Inhale. *Holy Spirit.* Exhale. *Comfort her.* And as I often do in prayer, I stopped praying words and prayed feelings. Pushing into the core of what I wanted without articulating it in my head. Inhale. Exhale.

There in that dark room, I created some quiet for someone else. A space to settle her spirit. To breathe in God's love and breathe out her need for him. And in settling into the darkness and

> There in that dark room, I created some quiet for someone else.

stillness, her body pressed against mine, her heart still pounding and her breath going strong, my prayers for her settled my own heart. Inhale. Exhale.

DAY 19

Today was the Sunday before Christmas.

My friend Kathy, whose love language is unquestionably gift giving, handed me a basket of treats at church with a note thanking me for helping in Sunday school during the year. The biggest gift in the basket was a book, *Soul Keeping: Caring for the Most Important Part of You*, with a note about how we care for little souls but we must not forget what *we* need.

As I flipped through the book on the way home (Derek driving, of course), I tried to ignore the typical backseat noise of fighting over who got to sit where and a thousand "I'm hungry" cries, quickly followed by "Do we have anything for lunch?" questions. I looked to see if there was something about quiet. What I found was a chapter titled "The Soul Needs Rest."

> Whether with an entire day, or periods of time set aside every day, your soul needs rest. Not a change of scenery or a spiritual retreat—those are fine and may *contribute* to rest. But to remain healthy, our souls need solitude with no agenda, no distractions, no noise.[6]

The contrast of the clamor inside the car with the suggestion of being alone with no distractions (no dishes to wash or emails to answer) and no noise (not a single other person, at least awake person, near me) was strong. A retreat sounded as likely as being on a reality TV show. Of the singing variety. In other words, never.

That kind of miracle doesn't just happen on its own.

DAY 21

Determined to make that miracle happen, I set the alarm for 6:00 a.m., my normal time to start getting our household ready for a Monday. But I had the benefit of winter vacation on my side. Kids would be sleeping in.

And I sat in the quiet. No agenda. And really no significant thoughts as I let the silence and the caffeine take over.

Sometimes for quiet to be prioritized, it must be scheduled.

DAYS 24-25

Christmas. No quiet happens for a mom on Christmas Eve or Christmas Day. Food to make, presents to wrap, guests to host, and packing to sleep over at grandparents'. Amid the added chaos, I tried to make a significant moment of quiet and reflection happen on Christmas Eve. I picked a children's book from our basket to read aloud to my crew in the glow of the tree's lights. No one cooperated. Santa was coming and the manger was no match.

Sometimes for quiet to be prioritized, it must be scheduled.

As I sat yelling the Christmas story over the heads of children running around the sofa and a husband who was telling everyone to get to bed, I realized I was the one who needed the moment, the quieting of my soul in the middle of the wrapping paper tornado that had hit our house. Breathe in. *Lord Jesus.* Breathe out. *Be present.*

DAY 26

The white Christmas we always hope for in Denver, but rarely get, happened. Now the night after the big day and the preparing and executing the machine of Christmas had come to an end. I realized so had all the meal planning. It was the day after Christmas and my family still needed to eat. So I walked to the grocery store by myself in the remains of the snowstorm.

As I walked home, it was dark, the cold hurt, and the snow fell. And it was quiet. I'm always surprised that everything seems quieter when it snows in the city. For two long blocks I was suspended in a winter fairyland with the silent flakes falling in front of me. I could see the Christmas lights on our front porch—the two strands that were working, anyway—beckoning me home on my two-block respite. And though the cold was fierce and my bags were heavy, I stopped in front of my house and watched the silent, lit-up scene inside. Because there was movement, I knew there was also noise, but I couldn't hear it. It was like a silent movie playing out in front of me.

And when I opened the door from the garage into the house, the noise hit. Quiet no more.

DAY 28

We went to church a few days ago, and my friend and pastor Jill shared about Simeon waiting for the Messiah.[7] And we talked about comfort in the long waits of nothing. Waiting for God to answer prayers. And often in the wait there is silence.

And I thought of the argument Derek and I had Christmas Eve as we were up too late putting out gifts for our kids. Only a few days later and I already didn't remember what the argument was about, but I did remember I went to bed not wanting to talk to him. Thinking, of course, how ironic it was that we were celebrating the birth of the Prince of Peace while having our own home-front battle. I'd draped a blanket of silence around me as a way to punish him.

Of the arguments I've had in the past, the most painful ones have involved silence. Because they imply giving up. Or worse, *You're not even worth my breath*. I would much rather have yelling, which at least shows passion. But silence always feels like a dismissal, a shutting out.

So as we had our signature "open mic" time at church after the sermon, when people are welcome to share how the topic of the morning is working out in their lives, I was reminded of the pain of silence from God. Sometimes quiet feels like you've been forgotten.

Whether in a marriage, or from a child who is estranged, or with an unanswered prayer. I needed this reminder that though I crave quiet now, there will be a day when quiet is the last thing I want. It will be an indication of an empty house, of my flock having flown the coop, of maybe even feeling forgotten. So as I cherish the quiet, I must learn to cherish the noise because I cherish from whom it stems.

DAY 30

Flipping through the *Spiritual Disciplines Handbook* again, I discovered another discipline: unplugging. Wait, what? Unplugging as a form of spiritual discipline? You mean this is a thing? Adele (as I like to refer to her these days) says, "Unplugging recognizes that personal beings are created for personal interaction by a personal God. We need to be in the presence of each other. Digital connections aren't enough to keep us healthy. We need to be touched. We need nonverbal signals. We need uninterrupted spaces in our lives for the presence of God and the presence of others."[8]

And I thought of Jesus. Who had to retreat from the people he did life with, his disciples, to have some quiet. After he fed a crowd of five thousand, he was tired. And he set himself apart. "Immediately Jesus made the disciples get into the boat and go on ahead of him to the other side, while he dismissed the crowd. After he had dismissed them, he went up on a mountainside by himself to pray."[9] And what I see here is that prayer is his replenishment. Not Instagram, the mindless TV, YouTube. It was speaking and listening to God.

I often feel like Jesus. Okay, not in the "God made flesh" way, but in the "everyone needing me" kind of way. The "exhausted crowds pressing against me, telling me they're hungry" kind of

> *As I cherish the quiet, I must learn to cherish the noise because I cherish from whom it stems.*

way. The "I need to go to a mountain retreat and pray to replenish" kind of way. It's no surprise that an unplugging is a spiritual discipline with a modern twist for the wired.

No matter the circumstance, we need space for quiet and prayer. Breathe in. *Holy Spirit.* Breathe out. *Your peace.*

What I Learned

Forcing quiet did force me to stop in many ways. There is no question cutting out social media made me more aware of my surroundings, the people and details right around me. I was able to lift my head from the screen, I had more free time (scary, in fact, how much more time I had), and I wasn't in a constant, low-pressure comparison game. For sure a win. But one I expected.

> No matter the circumstance, we need space for quiet and prayer.

What surprised me was how adding quiet increased my ability to tune in to what God was doing right around me. And more than anything how available he is moment by moment. I included a quote at the beginning of this chapter from Mother Teresa. Right before she said those words, she said, "We need to find God, and he cannot be found in noise and restlessness. God is the friend of silence."[10] Meditation and prayer were unexpected gifts that allowed for a continued conversation with God that wasn't full of me talking, as is typical of my prayer life, noisy that it is. But rather, gentle and continuous. Helping me to, yes, love my actual circumstances in the moment.

This was almost like my own little vacation or retreat from the world swirling around. Wait, I can control my environment some? I don't have to allow life to just happen, I can make some intentional decisions with the end in mind. And it worked. In fact, it makes me excited for the next month's experiment too.

Practices I'll Continue

Wake up while the house is still quiet.

Limit social media, especially on my phone.

Breath prayer for me and my children.

Turn off background noise.

Capture unexpected quiet.

Questions for Reflection

1. How much quiet (both literal and virtual) do you have in a typical day?
2. What challenges do you face when trying to implement quiet?
3. Does increasing silence impact how you experience God? If so, how?

Words for My Actual Life

Be still, and know that I am God. (Ps. 46:10)

MONTH 2

First Things First

Mornings

I'll tell you how the Sun rose—
A Ribbon at a time. . . .

—Emily Dickinson

The Need

A typical morning goes something like this:

6:00 a.m. Alarm on my phone sounds. I lie in my bed for a while, skim the Twitter feed on my phone, get up and make coffee.

6:30 a.m. Check on Gabi to see if she is awake.

6:45 a.m. Read email, check Facebook, get dressed, get Gabi fed. Some days Gabi's friend is dropped off by her mom, who is headed to work.

7:15 a.m. Drive Gabi (and friend) to middle school. Note: Derek is usually able to stay home while I do this, so everyone doesn't have to get in the car.

7:30 a.m. Return home. Make sure everyone else is up, general mayhem for an hour as we get breakfasts made (each girl with a different request, of course), school bags packed, Genevieve's lunch made, homework signed, hair brushed, clothes on, teeth brushed. I mentioned mayhem, didn't I?

8:30 a.m. Head out the door to drop off Genevieve at the elementary school and Gracelynn at the preschool. Lalo and I then move on to the rest of our morning.

It's not unusual to find me running through the house trying to find Lalo's lost matching shoe, deciding a shower may not happen, and letting the dream of smelling good and feeling presentable go. I then face the rest of my day frazzled from the rushed and overwhelmed pace I've set. I can't quite get organized, so the result is a constant state of dishevelment while playing catch up with my tasks and my time. Not to mention the guilt I carry from dropping someone off at school while yelling at her to "jump out of the car before the guy behind me honks again!" I'm too rushed to be present because I'm already behind.

Here's the truth: mornings set the tone for the day. Not just for me, but for my entire family. The better I am at starting my day, the more patient I am when the inevitable stressors pop up. It's also how I send my people out into the world, where they will likely be torn down a bit, so I want to launch them well. The more put together I feel, the more confident and calm I am, the better prepared I am to face the day.

The Experiment

This month I will focus everything on making mornings better. And by better I mean more peaceful, less chaotic, more streamlined. I may be busy, but I don't need to be frantic. I will be intentional about my first few waking hours to see if it improves my attitude and productivity the rest of the day.

My Actual Approach

Get up before the rest of my house.

Be fully dressed, makeup on before 8:30 a.m.

Streamline routines for breakfast prep and leaving the house.

DAY 1

We've established that in our house, there are two kinds of people: those who wake up and decide "the day's a-wasting" and those who need to ease into the idea of getting going. Some might call it morning versus non-morning people. We are a house divided. There is no question I am leader of the morning pack. With Gracelynn fully in my camp and Giulianna a hybrid of the two, depending on how enticing the activity Gracie has begun or the breakfast being served. Everyone else: easer-inners.

It seemed appropriate to hit this experiment as we started back to regular life after winter break. Back to the routines and delivering kids to three different schools at three different points in the morning. No more sleeping in; this was go time. And of course this very first morning Gabi stood at the fridge, her hand holding the door wide open while she looked inside. I could tell she was hoping some sort of lunch would jump out at her. I knew I hadn't helped the cause. There were sparse pickings when it came to lunch makings.

> A little forethought on the food and clothing front goes a long way.

Lunch stuff. I might just love mornings were it not for making lunches. I am always at a loss for what to put in, always feel like I don't have the right stuff. And why do they take so long to make?

So we got creative with the few rations we could find, and on the way home from dropping her off at school I stopped at the grocery store and stocked up. We were going to tackle lunches the right way, darn it! And we could even start with Genevieve's. I was home by 7:45.

DAY 2

I have two personas on the school playground: the pajama me and the done-up me. I drop off my kids in extremes. When I was going into the office more, my two selves were that much more noticeable because I wore heels on work days, so not only was I fancy, I was also two inches taller. But heels are rare now because, really, I can't wear socks with them and my feet get cold and they're just not practical. I guess that's what happens when one turns forty.

So on this morning after all the school drop-offs were made, I was headed to a work meeting. My recent cutting back made these less frequent, but they still happened one or two days a week.

Which meant more than pajamas as I walked out the door. But I was prepared. Day 2 and I'm learning the night before makes all the difference. When I woke up, half my work was already done. Lunches packed and in the fridge, kids' clothes and mine laid out, notes for my meeting on the kitchen island, ready to be grabbed as I walked out the door.

Everyone delivered to where they needed to be on time with no yelling. Well, isn't this nice? A little forethought on the food and clothing front goes a long way.

DAY 4

As we rushed out the door for our activities for the day, I was makeupless (remember the extremes) headed to my MOPS group. Where they know me and welcome my sweatpantsed self. Knowing that's where I was headed made the morning chaos a little more manageable.

Make time for preparing the house for the day.

Returning home at noon with my heart filled, I walked into my kitchen to bowls with milk and mushy cereal on the counter, coffee cups half full with the cream starting to separate, sandwich-making stuff still on the counter. And I realized the morning prep checklist needs to include leaving the house as I want to be welcomed home. The bed made, breakfast put away, counters wiped are a better greeting than a disaster.

Okay, noted. Make time for preparing the house for the day. I know myself well enough to know I will never—I repeat, never—hit perfection in the housekeeping realm, but I can have a bit of forethought as I start each morning.

DAY 6

Rare is the day when we need to be nowhere. Between school, church on Sundays, and soccer on Saturdays half the year, we almost always need to be somewhere by sometime. But the girls and I didn't this Saturday morning. Glorious!

Derek had a work event, and guess who was still in her pajamas when he got home at 1:00 in the afternoon? But guess what else happened? Emails were caught up, piles of clean laundry folded and put away, and the house cleaned by not only me but by four girls!

On this cold, snowy morning, all I wanted to do was hunker down. But that didn't mean we didn't have a beautiful time getting things done. There was a slower pace that is so rare for our family. I cherished the hours as they leisurely passed.

"Be still before the LORD" it says in Psalm 37.[1] How I want to stop and capture these moments when I know he is at work. If I am meant to be still in God's presence, and he is always present, then should I always be still? Given my actual life, that seems impossible, but maybe as still as this mother of four can. And maybe "still" looks like staying in pajamas on a Saturday.

DAY 8

I found a handwritten note on the kitchen counter. A little piece of paper with pencil writing that read

> Brekfest.
> Pack lunch.
> Brush hair.
> Git dressed.

A daily checklist for its author to follow. This one who is stressed about not having enough time in the mornings, who is an easer-inner, asked me to wake her up extra early so she could have more time to "wake up" (aka lie on the sofa and watch the rest of the house as it stirs) and tackle her new list. Absolutely! We all need to figure out how to make mornings work better for us. For me it's a "get 'er done" attitude. For this easer-inner, knowing she has plenty of time keeps it relaxing.

Done, my sweet.

DAY 9

Some mornings I have it all planned out and then a wrench gets thrown in. Today at about 7:15 I was strutting around like the house peacock, so proud of myself. I had prepped for the morning the night before and was headed to a coffee date after all the school drop-offs.

And then a last-minute work request arrived in my inbox. It needed to be done this morning. As in before I left the house. I stood in my kitchen, still in my pajamas, crafting and re-crafting words on my laptop as the minutes were ticking away. My masterful plan was crumbling. Peacock no more.

I glanced at the clock on the microwave and my hopes for a stressless morning disappeared. I was now late on all fronts. As I ran through the house screaming for everyone to get themselves dressed and in the car, Derek asked, "How's that experiment of yours going?"

"It's an experiment. Sometimes it works and sometimes it doesn't." The words came out like little arrows. I didn't care where they landed exactly, just as long as they were in his general vicinity.

"Oh." He smiled. There's nothing like a man of few words to eloquently make his point.

An hour later, as I sat in my car in the preschool parking lot, looking in the rearview mirror and applying my eyeliner, I realized it was all getting done. The kids were dropped off. I was almost going to be on time to my meeting. Breathe in. *Holy Spirit.* Breathe out. *Morning stress. It's going to be okay.* Being five minutes late was permissible, even acceptable with this friend.

My stress level was not matching the circumstances.

DAY 10

Many people start their day with their Bible, some coffee, and some prayer. A moment to recalibrate and get the day started right. I've bucked this "quiet time" formula for years because it feels too constraining, too much like this is the "right way" to connect with God. But as I age and mature a little, I'm realizing the wisdom in this approach. First, if you make that connection happen in the morning, it's done. Not in a checklist kind of way, but in a "I've connected through meditation, knowledge, and prayer with the maker of the universe" kind of way.

> Better to rest in him from the start than to run without him all day long.

And I remembered the premise of trying this experiment in the first place: Jesus always says come. Tired, overwhelmed, overjoyed. It doesn't matter. But especially the tired. He says, "Come to me, all you who are weary and burdened, and I will give you rest."[2]

As I feel the stresses of the day push down on me, tighten my neck muscles, make me short with my kids, I hear "Come." So I come this morning in the quiet hours and pray for his peace throughout the day. Knowing I will fall short. Knowing I won't be enough.

Better to rest in him from the start than to run without him all day long.

DAY 11

Half the battle with getting shoes and coats on in the morning is rummaging through all the layers of outerwear triple-piled on the hooks in our mudroom. We even have a mudroom, so we should be on top of the game with a designated space to grab what we want and run out the door. But the key component here is *organized*, and I simply am not that woman. (I had illusions of becoming her with motherhood because I thought all moms kept organized homes, but reality hit hard.)

Here is the problem: the mudroom is not only the place where things should easily be found as people walk out the door; it is also the place where everything is dumped when they return home. Six people walk through the garage at the end of the day, usually hungry, tired—and wanting to kick off their shoes. And so the younger variety do, right there, usually next to their designated shoe bin rather than in it.

I stood in the mudroom and looked at the soccer bags and raincoats taking up precious hook space and wondered why they were using up this real estate when it's clearly *not* soccer season and clearly time for parkas and gloves.

I'd just received a copy of my friend Kathi's new book, *Clutter Free: Quick and Easy Steps to Simplifying Your Space*. In it she says, "In order for something to earn a place on my kitchen counter, under the island in the middle of the kitchen, or in the cabinets, it needs to be used almost every day."[3] The items in my mudroom needed to earn their place for morning help. It was time to ask, "Do we need this every morning?"

So I said a prayer (because who knew what I would find in the piles), dove into the chaos of overflowing shoe bins and hooks that were about to be torn out of the wall from the weight of all that was stacked on them, and created a "give away" pile and a "store in much wiser location" pile. Here is what I cleared out:

12 coats (5 of them raincoats)

7 sweaters

7 extra backpacks/bags

2 lunch boxes

2 poodle purses (You know the kind. They look like poodles, but they're really purses. I wish we had only two in our house. We need a Claire's intervention.)

A pile of hats and mismatched mittens

After everything was put in their permanent homes, in closets and dressers and bedrooms, I stood in the mudroom and felt like I could breathe. And no joke, as I was standing there admiring

> When you think you have all that extra time, you really don't.

my fine organizational skills (it only took me an hour and a half to reorder the stuff accumulation), Derek opened the door from the garage and froze mid-step. Only his eyes moved, his hand still on the doorknob, as he took in the scene of decluttered space as if he was afraid to break the magic spell with any quick movements. His gaze landed on me and two words came out: "Praise Jesus."

DAY 12

Well, wasn't this nice to reach for a coat and find it? Gloves? Done. Only one pair per person in their basket instead of ten and a half.

School bags? Yes.

Soccer bags? No.

The time for getting shoes on and people out the door was cut by a third because we weren't combing through all the extras to get what we needed.

DAY 14

Sundays are notoriously hard mornings for us. You'd think because we all don't need to be in the car until 10:15 we'd be golden with all that extra time. However, it's the only day we all need to be leaving the house at the same time, and that seems to be a bit of a fiasco-maker.

Also, when you think you have all that extra time, you really don't.

DAY 15

Every morning I've been getting up and getting dressed, makeup on by the time I leave to take the girls to school. All in all a total of ten extra minutes to get a real outfit on. No yoga pants all day.

I'm finding I have a uniform. If I'm not much of a primper, I'm even less of a stylist. I don't know what the latest trends are. I completely trust my sisters-in-law to school me here. (Though my daughters are starting to have some opinions too.) I spend a lot of time on my feet during the day, so comfortable shoes are the one non-negotiable.

Hence the uniform has evolved. Every morning as I stare at my closet, I'm attracted to the same components: some type of skinny pants, a long shirt, boots, and a scarf. (For those reading this book in 2027, I know how dated this seems, but I promise I was not the only woman with this uniform.)

DAY 16

Lists! Lists are the key. All those organizational types always say that, right? That lists are vital to being on top of things. So I've started making them as early in the morning as possible. It clears my brain as I dump anything and everything I can think of that needs to be done (in my lifetime, practically) onto a sheet of paper. Even if I know it won't actually happen today, it helps me mentally, so I don't work to remember it. I know it's on the list.

Once I've written everything down, I break down bigger tasks. Clean the house? Do we have a week? No, I have to carve out smaller jobs:

Clean the bathroom.
Vacuum the bedrooms and hallway.
Do the dishes.
Clear the counters.

Why? Because the more specific we are in our tasks, the more likely we are to accomplish them so we can cross them off that list. Can we say satisfaction right there? Once I've created manageable jobs, I prioritize and put stars next to the three tasks that must get done today. When those are done I can star three more.

Sometimes I'll even rewrite the list, once everything is down, in categories of work type:

MOPS work.

Other work.

Writing.

House.

Kids.

I've even read making your list the night before helps clear your mind before you go to bed. That's a bit more organized than I can muster. Besides, I don't want to overdo it.

DAY 17

Right there in the Bible it says,

> GOD's loyal love couldn't have run out,
>   his merciful love couldn't have dried up.
> They're created new every morning.
>   How great your faithfulness!
> I'm sticking with GOD (I say it over and over).
>   He's all I've got left. (Lam. 3:22–24 Message)

His love and mercies are created new every morning. Whether it's in my morning routine or my need for forgiveness, every morning offers new hope for me. God will meet me where I am, regardless of my mood or circumstances. He offers new love. Every morning. He offers a new start. Every morning. I guess that's why I get the sense of possibilities.

DAYS 19–21

A stretch of days hunkering down at home. Below-freezing temperatures, work, and sick kids all kept me inside with an occasional run to the grocery store. And my experiment began to slip. No makeup. Greasy hair pulled into a ponytail. Every time I caught a glimpse of myself in the mirror, dark circles under my eyes staring back at me, I felt a little more discouraged. A self-perpetuating cycle.

My old ways were creeping back in, and with them some old feelings. Some lack of energy. Lack of motivation to take my life seriously. My day seriously. I was treating these days like throwaway days. I was falling into a rut.

DAY 21

I got up at 5:45 and determined things were going to be different.

A few hours earlier I'd woken up in Lalo's bed. Yes, me sharing a twin-sized bed, snuggled up to my pint-sized girl. I'd fallen asleep putting her down the night before and at 2:00 a.m. was still fully clothed, bra and all. I crawled out of her bed, stumbled into my room, and laid my fully clothed self in my own bed. As I closed my eyes I decided things were going to change. This was not restful. This was not thriving. This was on the verge of wretched.

By 7:00 I was showered, hair done, makeup applied, cutest work-around-the-house outfit I could come up with.

"Where are you going?" Gabi asked as I scrambled her eggs.

"Nowhere. I'm just tired of being sloppy."

My one big item on my day's agenda was a work call. I was a little nervous about the call, but the experiment was teaching me I would feel better about tackling it if I felt better about myself. And for me that meant clothes (the uniform), blow-dried and flat-ironed hair, makeup, coffee.

Besides, the mercies, the love, are created new every morning, right? I'll take full advantage of the fresh start offered today.

DAY 25

The email came last week. Other moms, the ones who are diligently at the school making all the extras happen, were looking for volunteers for Books and Bagels. I'm a bit of a shadow woman at my children's school. I'm not on the PTA. I don't volunteer in the classroom. I am happy to contribute to the teachers' gifts. My problem is remembering to bring the money to the playground to hand off to the diligent mom collecting it.

It's not that I don't think helping at the school is important. I do. But I tend to have two tag-along girls with me (not helpful distractions during third grade reading circles), and I simply can't commit to regular stuff because of my work schedule during the day and sports schedules in the evenings.

> Do what only you can do.

So when the email came in with the call for help for third grade Books and Bagels, I knew it fit my criteria: a one-time commitment, in Genevieve's classroom, and I could bring the littles with me.

I bought the juice and cream cheese a couple of days earlier when I was already at the grocery store, and I was going to have to take her to school regardless, so we just went an hour early and two little sisters marched into school carrying tubs of cream cheese.

I felt like Supermom, because I was doing something (but I wasn't doing everything). I could fully be present with Genevieve as she showed me her desk, as her teacher dumped a box of new books on the floor for kids to explore, as I cleaned up after giving the littles their jobs to do as they trailed behind me.

This was not an intentional part of my morning challenge, but the challenge had prepared me for it. And that was it. I felt I had made my contribution to the school for the year and I could check that demand off my list. Call me Slacker Mom, but I'm focusing on what I actually can do and not what I think I should do—or even worse, what I think others think I should do (that's like *should* two times removed).

Do what only you can do.

DAY 26

As I felt Lalo's forehead, I reverted to the office years of panic mode, trying to figure out if it would be acceptable for me to once again not go into work because of a sick child. Though I wasn't expected at an office this morning, I was expected at preschool. I'd signed up in August (yes, five months earlier) for all my helping days in Gracie's preschool class, and today was January's day. My mom was going to watch Lalo. I just needed to get everyone dressed, fed, and delivered to their proper destinations on time, and I was becoming an expert in that kind of strategic planning and delivery. But with his weakened immune system, Grandpa couldn't be around a feverish three-year-old. Morning plan thwarted.

> *My actual life has to allow for the reality of actual people.*

So I did what I often did when I was working in the office: I waited until the decent hour of 7:30 and began making phone calls to call in sick. My actual life has to allow for the reality of actual people. The people pleaser in me needed to recognize I have limitations. It was okay to cancel my morning plans.

DAY 29

I'm on a roll. Up and out of the house headed to my MOPS meeting. Fully showered. I wiped down the kitchen counters before I left. Everyone to school on time and I was even early to MOPS. I was motivated because I was meeting a friend who was visiting for the first time. I wanted to welcome her. The morning organization paid off once again, so I could be on time to be with someone important to me. Because that's the point of this whole experiment, right? To relish the people here today.

What I Learned

I was right, mornings do set the tone for the entire day. I can feel it for myself and for my people. Bringing some type of order to the morning chaos helps make everything run more smoothly.

Whether it's making the bed, cleaning the kitchen, or de-cluttering the mudroom, organization of stuff brings the frantic stress level down. And a list gives me some mental organization so I'm not looking at the next twelve hours without a few priorities in place.

Planning ahead is the number one way to make my mornings work. From going to the grocery store to have lunch stuff in the first place, to laying out clothes and packing bags and lunches the night before, anything that can be done the previous night is helpful. Keeping in mind that, no matter how much I plan, the unexpected can throw a wrench in things. So striving for better, not perfection, in this area is key.

How I feel about myself impacts my day. How I'm dressed impacts how I feel about myself. Therefore, how I'm dressed impacts my day and should be given proper attention. A uniform makes it easy; so does an automatic beauty routine. Nothing elaborate, but that push from blah to a little more color and an accessory or two makes me feel more put together and like I'm taking my life seriously.

Prayer in the morning grounds me in the truth of who I am at the beginning of each day. It's the carryover of quiet from last month into this one. A little coffee and quiet allows me to start the day the way *I* want to, rather than having the day and its craziness forced upon me.

Yay for mornings! And yay for coffee! Always.

Practices I'll Continue

Organize, prep, and lay out whatever I can the night before.

Wake up before the rest of my house.

Start my day with a prioritized to-do list.

De-clutter for the morning exit.

Have a fallback uniform that makes me feel put together (makeup a bonus).

Tidy up (especially the kitchen) before I leave.

Change plans when needed.

Questions for Reflection

1. Are you a "the day's a wasting" or an "easer-inner" when it comes to mornings? How about the people you live with? How does that impact your approach to this time of day?
2. What are three things you could try tomorrow morning that would help you have a more peaceful household?
3. If you believe God's compassion and mercies are created new every morning, how does that affect your outlook on mornings? On life?

Words for My Actual Life

His compassions never fail. They are new every morning. (Lam. 3:22–23)

MONTH 3

My Peeps

Dates

If on our deathbeds we were given an opportunity to reroll the videotape and do one aspect of our lives over, most of us, I am convinced, would pick our relationships—the chance to improve our connections with those we love the most.

—Richard A. Swenson

The Need

Mother of four, wife, daughter, friend, Sunday school teacher, soccer carpool driver, coworker, neighbor. These are all ways I describe myself. This is true of us as women, that when we are asked to describe the essence of who we are, we often do it through relationships. Because people are what matter most to us. If I had to pick one month in this nine-month experiment that I think is most important, it's this one. Because this is the whole point, right? To savor moments with my people!

Yet it's all too common to spend all day with these very people around me, at my feet, in my car, sitting at my kitchen bar, and still feel disconnected. Whether long days with a child at home where I feel isolated from the outside world, or rushing from work to school to church, the pace of my life can keep conversations at the logistical level of who is driving who, where, and when. I often choose texting over calling because I don't want to get over-involved in conversation; I just want to relay information. In the midst of the running around, the intimacies of friendship and marriage can be ignored.

I keep hearing that moms and dads feel rushed and have a hard time meeting the demands of their lives. I'm afraid in our world of choice we have more options in the work-life balance, but instead of saying no to some things to say yes to those we hold most dear, we are simply saying yes to everything, trying to cram more into our 24-hour days. The result? Our relationships are suffering.

The Experiment

I spend this month incorporating intentional one-on-one time with people I want to know and love better: my husband, my kids, my friends. From playdates to dates that require a sitter and reservations, I make time in my schedule to be present with the people I love.

My Actual Approach

Have one "date" per day with someone in my close circle.

Make casual interactions with strangers more personal.

Give others my undivided attention when they are speaking.

DAY 1

This seems like the easiest experiment so far. I've totally got this. I'm never alone. I am always with someone. So how hard will it be to spend some intentional time with the people I love?

Today I sat down at my computer to put some dates on the calendar and the colors popped up. Our family schedule, where every person has his or her own designated color, is like a rainbow of time. The more colors I see on the screen, the busier we are as a family, and the higher my stress level rises.

But I'm with these people all day long, so, really, how hard will it be to build in some dates? I looked at the calendar again and saw no evening, no afternoon, no significant block of time to plan anything with *anyone*. I needed to be cutting, not adding here. My initial enthusiasm for this month's experiment moved to instant discouragement. All I could think of were the famous words of comedian Jim Gaffigan on parenting four kids: "You want to know what it's like having a fourth? Imagine you're drowning . . . and then someone hands you a baby."[1]

I'm drowning.

"Mom, have you seen my backpack?"

"Mom, I'm hungry."

"Mom!!"

As I stared at the computer screen, hoping something would miraculously shift on our family's schedule to make this work, the very people I was trying to allow more time for interrupted me. I stood up and moved on to figuring out what snacks I could hand out. Apparently putting a few things on the calendar is not as easy as I'd imagined.

DAY 2

Gracie started ballet tonight. At a little rec center in the suburb just to the west of us. As I drove to the address, I recognized the block and a favorite restaurant across the street. Lalo and I walked Gracie into her class, her leotard on, her hair braided, and her ballet slippers in hand. She was nervous and I was excited for her.

> *I'm finding I'm mining the treasured moments out of each day.*

"Parents," the teacher in her grown-up-sized leotard said, addressing the other tall people in the room, "my policy is you must leave during class time. It's too distracting if you are here."

I looked down at Giulianna. Neither of us liked the idea of being kicked out, but we suddenly had a built-in date hour. We walked across the street to the restaurant with its windows facing right into Gracie's classroom and ordered drinks and a snack.

Things were looking up. Monday nights just officially became date nights. I had visions of laughter and meaningful conversation for Mondays on end as I brought a different person with me each week. I now have a master plan to multitask with my date time too. That's really how it's going to happen.

DAY 4

Derek and I have never been a "date night" couple. We've found it a bit cheesy, a bit formulaic, and therefore confining. We pride ourselves on going with the moment. Being more present in the everyday. Valentine's Day is coming up. Who needs it? It's for amateurs, those who limit romance to one day a year. We're kind of smug that way.

Besides, the cost of a babysitter on top of dinner often makes the idea of going out feel way out of budget. So we've mastered the date night in. Our kids will be quiet for ninety minutes with a movie. When they were smaller I'd try to manipulate naptime to make for early bedtime. Now that they're older the promise of a movie if they eat before us is compelling enough to make them comply.

But right now I wish we were date night people. Because our communication is happening in texts. So it's time to push the smugness aside and make a "date night" happen. Because I love this man and I want to spend time with him in more than three sentence increments and with real facial expressions and not just emojis.

DAY 5

> Could you pray for Molly? She's at Children's Hospital and about to have her appendix taken out.

It was a group text from Kristi. I pictured Kristi's family, all six of them in the familiar Children's ER. I also pictured the boredom and hunger that were likely taking over her non-adult troops.

> Who is with you? Do you need me to come pick up kids?

I texted back without considering what was on our family schedule for the next few hours. Sometimes you need to wipe the schedule clean when crisis mode hits.

A few hours later another of Kristi's friends pulled into my dark driveway and dropped off three kids carrying backpacks and pillows. Our evening plans for dinner and bed had been hijacked. I was loving my friend by caring for her kids because that's what we do for each other. I'd given her plenty of opportunities to do the same when my girls were in Children's Hospital.

My dates today were unexpected with three kids who needed reassurance that their sister was okay and school would be waiting for them as it always was in the morning. Not what I had planned, but I'm finding I'm mining the treasured moments out of each day.

DAY 8

I looked out the window to see the snow falling and wondered if we'd make it to church. A new study conducted at the University of London and released in the *American Journal of Epidemiology* concluded that being part of a religious group is the secret to sustained happiness. "The researchers noted that it is unclear whether the benefits of participating in a religious organization are connected to being in the religious community, or to the faith itself."[2]

Is it the faith or the people? I'm not sure I need to separate the two. My faith is intertwined with my people. Those I live with and those in my circle of support. People made in God's image, each of whom gives me an insight into who he is, to what hope looks like. It's that larger community that has held me up in my lowest points.

For this reason I make church a priority. I could listen to sermons online (which I sometimes do) or sing my heart out in worship alone (which I also sometimes do, usually in the car, which makes for interesting stoplight moments). But standing next to the same people week in and week out, people from whom I cannot hide, who ask and truly want to know how I am doing—this sustains me in a different way.

I like how Tara M. Owens describes the Sunday gathering process in *Embracing the Body.*

We witness the work of God in one another, not just in the singing of songs or the words of the pastor, but in the weekly way we bring our bodies together. We may not touch physically, but we coagulate, binding the wounds the world has inflicted on us during the week, drawn together by the redemption call of Christ, the One for whom we all long.[3]

So though there were a million reasons why it would have been easier to not go to church—it's snowing, we'd rather stay in our pajamas all day, we don't want our kids to get the germs in Sunday school during flu season—we went. Because we needed to coagulate. Because there is something about actually standing next to someone that makes a difference. That physical presence that can't be duplicated in a chat or Facebook thread. Because my dates are with my larger group.

DAY 9

Monday night. Ballet night. Happy hour night.

I convinced Genevieve to come with me. The promise of cheese fries is compelling. She had her homework. I had my work. We sat and didn't talk much. We read. Snacked. Checked in. Worked some more.

I have the urge to capitalize on every moment. To make it count. To fill it with words and activity. I've always associated connecting with talking, but sometimes I'm just contributing to the noise of my life. Sometimes my kids tune me out because I'm contributing to their noise too.

This second child, who thrives on one-on-one time, didn't need me to talk. She wanted to be with me. So I let it sink in, this picture of one-on-one in my brain. I prayed as I flipped through the notebook in front of me that she would impress this time on her heart too. That quality time can be next-to-each-other time.

> *Quality time can be next-to-each-other time.*

65

DAY 11

Alex
Lunch?

Jen
Yes, please!! Where can I meet you??

Whole Foods?

Yip. What time?

Now.

I missed my friends. I knew today was Jen's day off from work and preschool was close to her house, so I sent a text as I waited in the preschool pick-up line. It was an off chance that she was free to drive down the hill to meet us, but it wouldn't happen unless I asked.

I've never heard someone regret making people a priority over work. Not if they have people around them to love. Even if your work is caretaking, teaching, or counseling, if you have your own clan, who love you without end, they are your priority. Yet for me at least the immediate reigns. I need to make this phone call, write this email, make this meal. Yes. All things that need to happen, but how do I prioritize in a way that makes me notice the PEOPLE. RIGHT. IN. FRONT. OF. ME! I don't know how to not just give this lip service, but truly absorb it. Practice it. I need to scream it right back to myself.

But perhaps it's one invitation at a time. One moment at a time.

> *Perhaps it's one invitation at a time. One moment at a time.*

DAY 12

My friend Meghan says, "Life is big in the little." She's from Tennessee, so when I first heard her say that I thought it was some Southern phrase like "The Big Easy." But no, it's more literal. She explains, "It's not what you do; it's how you do it."

In other words, we can be cleaning a kid's room (one of our least favorite activities around here because the rooms can feel like a scary jungle as we risk life and limb to climb through the mess, and, well, because kids hate cleaning them because they are kids), and have meaningful conversation or just a little fun. I'm the one who is often setting the tone in the wrong direction. My frustrations creep in. *Why don't these kids take care of their things?!* or *Who do they think is going to clean up after them?! Me?* The potential shared time is still shared. It's just not fun.

> *It's not about having time; it's about making time with the right attitude.*

It's not about having time; it's about making time with the right attitude. Right here in the little.

DAY 13

Derek and I were attending the same luncheon downtown today, so we did what other mobile working couples do: we put our offices (aka our computers) in our respective bags and got in one car when the sitter arrived. We drove downtown, parked near the Convention Center where we'd be having lunch, and walked to a hotel across the street. (No, this is not going where you think it is.) We ordered some coffee and sat in the lobby facing each other, both of our computers open.

Not many words were shared. Sometimes just being close to each other feels like a reconnection. Where I can glance up from my computer screen and see him there with his halfsie reading glasses, looking dapper. An older version of the young man I fell in love with nearly twenty years ago. This life we share is beautiful despite all its chaos.

DAY 16

Ballet night. Happy hour night. My heart sank a bit when Derek said he wanted to take Gracie to ballet so he could work during her class time (away from our noisy house). My perfect plans once again thwarted by the very people I want to spend time with. Oh, you mean they have their own perfect, yet different plans too? Dang it.

DAY 18

Because I'm an introvert, a day when I can stay home feels like respite. But there is one group of people I force myself to be with. Not because it's torture to be with them (quite the opposite; I love it), but because I am better after having spent time with them: my MOPS group.

As a writer, I can get over-involved in my own head. I think about words, ideas, things I want to say, and then sit at my computer and type away. In a sense, feeling like I'm having a conversation because I'm stringing together sentences to convey what I am trying to communicate to an audience of people.

But writing is a one-way conversation and can be used as a place to hide. I need people, real-life people, who accept me with my bad breath and whose bad breath I accept. I need the rub of being annoyed and annoying. I need flesh and blood to listen to the tone of my voice, wipe the tears, give me a hug. But I need to be all that for others too.

The truth is, it's easier for me to hole up and communicate with the outside world through my various screens. But texts and Instagram posts can't replace the nitty-gritty of real people. Even for an introvert. And so I pushed myself out of my comfortable hiding places and headed to my MOPS meeting. Because it's good for me to coagulate.

DAY 19

I see clearly that the thing the church needs most today is the ability to heal wounds and to warm the hearts of the faithful; it needs nearness, proximity.

Pope Francis[4]

This proximity idea got me thinking. God tells us to draw near to him and he will draw near to us.[5] In fact, he came to earth wrapped in skin, the world's largest mystery, as Jesus, to demonstrate his love for us.

How does that play out for our flesh and blood people? The ones we can wrap our arms around and touch? Who scratch and bite and poop? If we draw close to them, as in snuggle in on the couch, slide closer on the dining room bench, touch them as we talk, will they draw near to us?

DAY 20

Derek came home with a stack of property fliers in his hand. He placed them on the table and I knew what he'd been doing. He'd been driving around, perhaps headed to a meeting or maybe out with the purpose of looking at properties, and a "For Sale" sign caught his eye.

He's been talking for months about the possibility of Providence Network, where he serves as the executive director, opening a new home for young adults coming out of homelessness. And proximity is what "Prov," as we call it in our house, specializes in. Creating communities for people coming out of addictions, domestic violence, homelessness. Creating safe places to rebuild their lives. Where many of the staff members live in the homes with the residents. Because life isn't done on shifts or schedules. Recreating family is done at all hours and in all circumstances.

And it's done within the context of home. Talk about proximity.

So my husband has been scouring the city looking for the perfect property. One that would meet the needs of the staff and residents in both structure and location. One that would make sense with the neighbors at hand. That would be a wise use of Prov's limited funds—money, in fact, that still needed to be raised. I could see the stress on his face. The determination to keep going, to do the good he is called to in the world, to offer young people a second (or maybe third or fourth) chance. Because it is the right thing to do. And because he can.

I walked up to him and wrapped my arms around him, giving this man, who makes me feel safe when he does the same to me, my best five-foot-two version of a bear hug.

DAY 21

Our neighbor texted,

> Can the girls come over and play? I have one
> who would really like it.

By the girls I knew she meant the littles.

I was at the library working, so I told her to go over and knock on our kitchen window because Derek was working in the basement. The bigs were having an impromptu sleepover at their grandparents'. There was no question those two littles were home and would love to spend the late afternoon next door.

A few hours later I texted Derek,

> **Alex**
> Do you want me to stop at the store for dinner?

> **Derek**
> The littles are having pizza next door, so it's
> only us. What do you want?

I was practically giddy. We now had an empty house, only ourselves to consider when deciding what to eat, and better yet what to talk about. It was a full-fledged date right in our very kitchen.

The littles inevitably walked across the street before our dinner was ready, but we simply put on a movie for them, sat at the table, and talked. Uninterrupted. Not rushed. Every once in a while we are handed this gift of time. It's up to us to take it.

DAY 24

Gabi sat next to me in the minivan as I drove her to basketball. I could have asked her about friends at school. About the game we were headed to. About her distaste for brussels sprouts. Anything! But I didn't. A missed opportunity.

And then I thought of both proximity and quiet. Maybe this girl just needs to know I'm willing to drive her to the other side of the city during rush hour in the winter for her to play a basketball game. Maybe I don't need the conversation to be connecting. Maybe I need to take some of the pressure off myself in this "quality time" experiment and live life with her and not have every encounter lead to the most meaningful, memorable conversation ever!

> *Every once in a while we are handed this gift of time. It's up to us to take it.*

Or maybe I'm trying to make myself feel better and it was a missed opportunity.

DAY 25

Tonight, as I sat down on the couch in front of the TV and Genevieve automatically slid across the sofa so she could be right next to me, like she was under some type of magnetic pull, I wasn't surprised. Because one of her love languages, as best I can tell, is physical touch. She is a snuggler.

I wondered if I needed to be intentionally connecting with my kids the way they are naturally wired to receive love. (The basic premise of the book *The 5 Love Languages* is—you guessed it—there are five different ways to connect with people.) I even had a copy of *The 5 Love Languages of Children*. I bought it years ago, and went down tonight to recover it from my basement office.

Of course it is good to feel love and to verbalize it, but this is not sufficient to make a child feel loved unconditionally. The reason for this is that children are behaviorally motivated. They respond to actions—what you do with them. So to reach them, you must love them on their terms, or behaviorally.[6]

In other words, I need to show them love in a way that's meaningful to them, not just tell them with my audible voice a thousand times a day (though I don't think that ever hurts).

DAY 26

"I think this might be the one." Derek walked into the kitchen and placed a flier on the counter. The property that just might work. We'd been praying, believing God cares about these kinds of details, and Derek had surely done his due diligence in searching.

Our conversation unfolded as I made dinner and he recounted his day.

I needed to be intentionally connecting with my kids the way they are naturally wired to receive love.

If it goes right, this part of the day is one of my favorite connection points: me making dinner, him sitting at the kitchen bar facing me with a drink, us talking. Our family noise in the background. Kids are getting homework done, watching TV, getting picked up for soccer carpool. This is not the glamorous night out, but it's an average night in with the people I love. I've heard it called the witching hour because kids are often tired and beginning to unravel, and the challenge of getting dinner on the table amid the chaos is real. But like I said, if it goes right . . .

"No interruptions," Derek commanded, mostly to the air because the children the words were intended for continued to make noise about something. We try to enforce this reconnection time, almost never with total success. But 50 percent success is better than nothing.

I determined to focus on what he was saying and shut out the rest of the family clamor as I chopped the carrots.

DAY 27

"Mom, can I have a playdate at Daisy's house?" I was on the school playground to pick up Genevieve from school and she wanted to go home with her friend instead.

Well, this was a waste of time, I thought. *Why did I drag two littles into the car, drive down here, now with half an hour to waste before needing to go pick up Gabi from practice after school, when I could have been at home attending to the 3,251 things that need to get done?! There is not enough time for me to waste like this!* Frustration easily mounts in my head.

"Yes," I said. Because why shouldn't my girls have dates be a priority in their lives this month too?

And then Heather walked over and I relaxed a bit. I hadn't seen my friend in a while. My sweet friend, who is parenting alone since her husband, Jon, died two and a half years ago. Heather, who I always want to encourage, always want to hang out with, and for whom I never seem to have enough time to make my intentions reality.

"I went to grief counseling today," she said. We sat down right where we were, on the edge of a concrete planter, and made space for the updates and the hugs while our kids circled around us. The "I'm hungry" and "Can we go?" cries beckoned us to get up and move, but this time together was so rare, we blocked out the whining and focused on each other.

As I drove to the middle school, the next stop in my afternoon's route, I thought, *Not a waste of time at all.*

There is something about being open to the person God puts in front of us and putting our own agendas aside. I still needed to leave to pick up Gabi at a certain time, but I could fully use those few minutes by sitting with my friend and listening.

In fact, Jon, Heather's husband, is a great reminder to me that people are my priority, because every single day with them really is a gift. It can be so cliché, this thought of seizing the moment, but when you are with a friend who would love to recapture some of the moments, to go back in time to be with someone who is no longer here, the glaring truth that life is fleeting is unmistakable.

God of all healing counsel! He comes alongside us when we go through hard times, and before you know it, he brings us alongside someone else who is going through hard times so that we can be there for that person just as God was there for us. (2 Cor. 1:3–4 Message)

> *My truest calling as a follower of Jesus is to love God fully and others fully.*

I will never be able to give Heather what she truly wants, her husband back. But I can offer my prayers on her behalf, trusting God to meet her with what she needs. I ask myself what I can do in this moment that will make a difference. What can I offer her with what I have right now?

My truest calling as a follower of Jesus is to love God fully and others fully. How much more can I show that than by giving them my full attention when present with them?

DAY 28

Can I count this as a total failure of a month if I didn't go on a single traditional date with my husband? (And it was even Valentine's Day.) Good intentions don't always result in desired outcomes. Argh.

Had I put it on my rainbow-colored calendar that first day, it would have occurred, since—surprise—actually putting things on the calendar helps make them happen. But the overwhelmedness of adding one more thing got the best of me. Rocket science here, people. Rocket science.

What I Learned

Though intentional, planned dates are valuable—even special—these days, they can't carry the bulk of my relational time. Maximizing the built-in opportunities I have every day to connect with the people around me makes the most significant difference. They really are what will affect my actual life and my actual relationships. Whether it's meeting someone for a spontaneous lunch hour or three minutes on the sofa at our house or anywhere in between, *opportunities* is the best word I can muster for these moments. Because there is an active choice in whether I take advantage of them.

> *It's small decision after small decision to be present.*

It has helped to remember physical nearness matters, and I can be more available with my attention if I am actually in other people's presence. So it makes sense that the more time I spend with someone, the more opportunities we will have to connect (and then again it is my responsibility to say yes to those opportunities when they do come up). At the same time, spending more time together releases some of the pressure as a mom, wife, and friend to have every encounter be epic. It's the age-old debate about which is better, quantity or quality time. And the best answer I can muster is that it's a combination of both.

Though my schedule is tremendously full, my time with people can be relished by simply stopping and recognizing the opportunities in front of me. It's small decision after small decision to be present. Stop. Breathe. Focus on the face God has placed in my path.

Practices I'll Continue

Schedule time in my calendar to be with specific people.

Take a child (or friend or husband) with me on an errand or to a practice.

Invite someone to coffee or lunch that same day.

When possible, connect with people physically instead of virtually.

Actively participate in my church community.

Be present with eye contact and listening ears with whoever is right in front of me.

Questions for Reflection

1. Who would you like to spend more time with on a regular basis? What is keeping you from making that happen?

2. Do you have a regular time in your schedule when you are waiting or driving that could double as date time with someone?

3. Do you find it more difficult to make quantity or quality time happen with those you love? What are three small changes you can make today to take advantage of your date opportunities?

Words for My Actual Life

Come near to God and he will come near to you. (James 4:8)

MONTH 4

Being Kind to My Body

Health

You're in pretty good shape for the shape you are in.

—Dr. Seuss

The Need

Years. That's the last time I went for a routine checkup (apart from having babies, of course). Exercise? Inconsistent at best. Sleep? Too often limited to the hours between midnight and 6:00 a.m. It's not a stretch to conclude the lack of care for my body is impacting all areas of my life. I use food as comfort, not as energy. I don't make sleep a priority because I can always just drink more coffee to make up for the exhaustion.

Part of my excuse is I'm taking care of everyone else, right? We women are drawn to caretaking and yet we are notorious for putting our own health needs on hold while we attend to those around us. (I make it a priority to take my children to their doctor visits regularly, so why can't I make it to mine?) This becomes a self-perpetuating cycle of exhaustion and poor health, keeping me from having the energy to savor every day. How can I appreciate what's right in front of me when all I can think about is how tired I am?

And I would be telling an incomplete story if I didn't confess there is a whole lot of vanity wrapped into my motivation on this month's experiment too. My body is changing, and I can either figure out how to live within the changes or resent them. I truly want to be a woman who ages gracefully, embracing my current stage of life. But I fear I'm headed in the opposite direction, resenting every growing curve.

Based on both my own and my friends' general state of exhaustion, I'd say this burning it at both ends is becoming a cultural norm. *Women's Health* magazine featured an article titled "Why

Are Modern Women So Exhausted?" The author concludes our 24/7 "on" is putting us in constant fight-or-flight status. Small doses of the stress hormone cortisol can motivate us, give us that natural boost, but when it is constant our bodies are worn down. "Staying continuously restless means the body never returns to a calm baseline state—it's been rewired to be all stress response, all the time."[1] Our always "on" mentality is creating mobile stress centers otherwise known as our bodies.

Guilty on all counts. One thing's for sure, I know I can do better here.

The Experiment

This month I make my physical care a priority. From maintaining a regular bedtime to consistent exercise, I'm going to step over the mommy-guilt and make time for my body.

My Actual Approach

Exercise for twenty minutes four days per week

Drink at least four 8-ounce glasses of water per day

Get eight hours of sleep a night

DAY 1

I *need* this! Oh, I've needed the first few months of experiments too, but I *need* this.

For months I'd been doing a ten-minute video workout regimen. Well, sporadically at least. Ten minutes seemed to work well in my schedule. But a few months ago I got a new computer and it didn't have a DVD player, so I bought an attachment for the computer that would play the videos and then I couldn't find the attachment. It was all getting too hard and became enough of a barrier to put a halt to my already measly ten-minute efforts. So today I feel bleh. Low energy, yet restless. I *need* this.

I went out to the garage at 6:15 a.m., removed the Christmas tree stand from the treadmill where it was being stored (yes, it's March), and walked for fifteen minutes, even ran for a few. But let's not go overboard. The goal is health, not torture.

DAY 2

Every day I look in the mirror and see my face, my hair, my body changing. I had it good for about 39.5 years. My body produced four beautiful babies. My belly stretched across state lines, because this short-torso girl had nowhere to go but out. And after each one of my girls emerged, nursing did its calorie-burning magic and I was back to size tiny.

But it's as if my body knew I'd had it good and easy for too long and said, "Forty's approaching; it's time we make her feel it a bit." And that metabolism came to a screeching halt.

And my skin. I developed pregnancy mask with my third pregnancy, pigment in my face creating darkish spots. And it returns when I'm out in the sun. The best part is that it creates a mustache-like appearance on my upper lip. Ladies at the makeup counter have agreed it's a problem, just one they can't fix. I see the lines in my face that don't go away when I relax.

Reality bites.

DAY 3

I lied. I have had one doctor's appointment in the last year; I had a mammogram six months ago right when I turned forty. My motivation was my mother. Not that she's a breast cancer survivor; she just kept asking me about it. Sometimes our moms take care of us even when we're forty.

Then a second mammogram because the first had some "irregular calcification." You want to know what dread feels like? Sitting in a breast cancer center, the one where you go for your follow-up mammograms, and look at the faces around you. And then I realized the terrified face next to me was Derek's second-cousin-or-other and we clung to each other like long lost relatives (which we kind of were).

I've now lived long enough to know friends who were "too young" when they died. I can't let my age, or my busy schedule, keep me from giving my body attention. Blowing it off is an option, just not a wise one.

All to say I need to have a mammogram every six months for three years. My letter came today to schedule my next one.

Called. Check. Done.

DAY 5

I am determined to make the workouts happen. So today I got the exercise uniform on. (I have learned the power of the uniform.) And then the girls wanted breakfast and needed to be driven to school, and work emails needed to be answered and laundry folded. Maybe it was subconscious procrastination. Who am I kidding? Of course it was. I'm surprised the toilets didn't get cleaned and next year's taxes done a year early so I could avoid the treadmill. I guess a little potential discomfort goes a long way for my avoidance techniques to kick in.

> *I can't let my age, or my busy schedule, keep me from giving my body attention.*

When I picked the big girls up from school and still had my yoga pants on with no yoga to show for it, I knew I couldn't put off a few minutes of exercise any longer. Besides, they were watching me. They know what this month is about. If I expect them to care for their bodies, I need to step it up a little and do the same for mine.

We pulled into the driveway and I walked straight into the garage and to the treadmill, where I used it for twenty minutes. It wasn't that bad. Really. And the satisfaction once it was done was worth it.

There is no magic to making self-care happen. I just have to start.

DAY 6

I'm sore from my treadmill activities. I might have been embarrassed by this detail ten years ago, that such mild physical activity could be considered stress on my sedentary body, but I'll take it as evidence that I'm doing something right. Moving my body in a different way.

To be sore when I stand up from my computer or walk across the room reminds me what a miracle it is in the first place to have this shell of flesh and bone to move through the world. No one else is going to take care of this body for me. I'm in charge of this one.

DAY 7

I haven't slept well in over thirteen years. Since my first pregnancy. One night in our little house in Portland, I tossed from side to side, thinking how uncomfortable I was. It was 2:00 a.m. and Derek lay next to me asleep (oh, the thoughts that go through a pregnant woman's mind about how her husband has it so easy). And then Derek began to twitch next to me. A twitch that turned into convulsing. He's only experienced it one other time in our marriage, a seizure from low blood sugar. A call to 911, paramedics, a shot. A reminder that his body does not work on autopilot as mine does.

There is no magic to making self-care happen. I just have to start.

My husband has had to manage his health since he was nine years old, when he began to "manage his diabetes." He is my model for having more to think about than the occasional pass on the chocolate cake. His body requires more attention to function in the day to day. And yet he manages it so under the radar that I often forget it's an issue.

So that night of pregnancy when tossing and turning with hot feet and pillows stuffed between my legs kept me up was the beginning of sleepless years. Not because of Derek, though that night is memorable, but because of our children. We've had a child or two with us in our room ever since. Either in my belly, in a bassinette, or squeezed between us in our bed. Not because of intentional co-sleeping philosophy, but simply because it's easier to roll over and let the girl crawl in than to fully wake up taking her back to her room. To this day, we often have at least one child come into our room in the wee hours of the night and snuggle close or lie on the floor.

But I will always take this reason for the sleeplessness over the alternative. One night when Gabi was about three years old, I lay in bed wondering why she was allotted more space in the bed than I was and then imagined her as a sixteen-year-old, refusing to talk to me, much less letting me touch and snuggle and cuddle her. I determined then that these snuggles are fleeting. I will miss this someday. I will miss the middle of the night tuck-ins after nightmares or sheets being changed because of accidents. They won't always be here.

Sometimes I just need to remember that now. This. These moments are exactly what I want. But I'm still tired.

DAY 8

Derek took the littles to Linda's community room dedication. Linda, an integral part of the Providence Network community. To understand what Linda does you must understand Prov. A collection of houses and apartment buildings where people in recovery, escaping violence and homelessness, live together in intentional community. Linda is the director of one of these apartment buildings. Linda has been dying this year.

And with her dying she has had a series of markers to acknowledge the gifts in her life while she is still able to enjoy them. She had a big picnic party last summer with two hundred of her closest friends. Music and face painting and the host's dog ate the cake. It was perfect.

But today Derek and the littles attended a smaller party, mostly people who have worked closely with her or have lived with her.

They celebrated her influence in the Prov community and dedicated the community room of the apartment building to her. This space where she hosted Broncos-watching events and birthday parties. Since she realized the severity of her breast cancer recurrence, and that she had a few months left to live, her daily posts on Facebook have been titled "Grieving Grateful." The grief of having to say good-bye and the gratefulness for the details that have made up her life. These posts have been a wonderful prompt for all of us to relish what's right in front of us.

Linda has been reminding me our bodies are but temporary. I have not walked someone close through to death. I certainly have known people who have died, but I haven't been the one to hold their hand and hear what it is to live their last days. Linda has been giving me a peek into the heart of someone who is approaching death with a grateful spirit.

DAY 11

"Who wants to go to Sweet Cow later?" I threw the question over my shoulder to the van's passengers while on our drive home from church, pretty sure this offer to walk to the neighborhood ice cream shop would secure me the title of fun mom for the day. I got three enthusiastic yeses and one "I'm not feeling well." That one I so wanted to please, to shake out a bit of the tween-ness, but I had to give her space, let her know I wanted to spend time with her, but not force it. Because forced fun is never really fun.

So I took three girls on a walk through the neighborhood. And canceled out any health benefits of the exercise with the ice cream I ate.

DAY 12

Six to eight cups. That's the standard water prescription for us to drink. And I've been dehydrated my whole life. Give me coffee. Give me beer. Give me Diet Coke. No problem. But *water*? I'm terrible at it. My girls ask for about 3,247 cups a day each. And every time I'm bewildered.

I had contractions with my last two pregnancies way earlier than was good for arrival time. Diagnosis: dehydration.

So this month I'm making myself drink water. I drink it in the morning before coffee. In the afternoon before the Diet Coke. At night with dinner. Last night I even busted out some Pellegrino. If I'm going to do water, making it fancy makes it more fun. (Don't tell me if it's not as good for me. I want to enjoy every little bubble down to the last drop.)

DAY 14

As I stood up today, I felt my knee give a little. That hobble made me more aware of my knee than I've been in weeks. And as I thought about all the ways I'm dependent on that knee, I appreciated it more than I had in a long time. I guess that's true of all my physical deficiencies a bit. They make me more aware of my body, so I can better appreciate how it works.

The changes in my body I resist, even resent, can point me toward what a gift I actually have.

DAY 15

I've noticed my eyes getting worse the last six months. Just yesterday I couldn't tell what Genevieve was eating across the room. I just knew it was a bowl of something white. A little hard to discipline when you can't see. "Stop eating . . . well, whatever it is! Dinner is in *ten* minutes!"

The changes in my body I resist, even resent, can point me toward what a gift I actually have.

I wasn't even sure if our insurance covered vision, so of course I texted Derek (Mr. Contacts) because he'd know. Costco. That's where he goes to get his eyes checked. Because why not see an optometrist while picking up enough toilet paper for a year and some tires for your car? The good news is, I know Costco. Called. Appointment made for Friday. I could have done this years ago.

DAY 17

I was determined to exercise in the morning. Determined. Before I could be distracted by the pull of my daily duties, I got on the treadmill and turned on the TV. Rachael Ray was the woman of the hour, and since I can't figure out how to change the channels on the television in the garage, it was Rachael or silence.

As I walked on the treadmill, I watched a makeover take place with a woman who'd lost almost one hundred pounds in the last year. And over and over, Rachael, this woman, and that guy from *What Not to Wear* talked about her curves. How her curves have changed, come out, been unveiled almost, as her body has lost some layers. It was like a sculptor making a shape out of a massive piece of stone. The curves were being revealed and she was overjoyed to show them off.

The message that the curves were a good thing, that she was a woman made to have them, clanged against my attempt to make all things flat.

I moved from the treadmill to the garage floor, doing sit-ups now, trying to flatten my torso. How am I embracing my body? My changing body? Granted, hers was changing in the direction she wanted, but if health is my goal and my curves are still there, the ones I *don't* want to accentuate, how do I love what I have today?

A memory of this very spot from a year earlier rushed back to my mind. Standing in the garage talking to my neighbor, she put her hand on my belly and lowered her voice to almost a whisper. "Is that a baby bump I see?" I could tell she was genuinely excited about the possibility of another Kuykendall on the block. I, on the other hand, was mortified. Trying to act nonchalant about the whole thing, I answered, "Oh, it's a baby bump all right, four babies later. But no, I'm not pregnant."

I continued my sit-ups.

DAY 18

I found it! Last night I found the DVD thingy that attaches to my computer and I pulled out the familiar "ten minutes" DVD. With girls pulling on the exercise bands I was trying to use, I started as I so often have with the first segment: upper body. Rubber band wrapped around my living room post, I followed the instructions commanded from the computer screen. The littles played under bands, pulled on them, and then thought they'd be helpful by guiding my arms through the motions with their own little hands.

> *Taking care of my body is not just for my benefit. It also gives those I love the best version of me I can offer.*

"Please don't." I was short and to the point. They pulled on the bands again.

"I said, 'Please don't.' It makes it harder for me." Catching my stern tone, I decided for the self-deprecating approach. "It's already hard enough." I kept pulling the bands up and down, the burning in my triceps moved from subtle to full-fledged.

Lalo pointed out to Gracie how funny the man on the computer sounded, and I realized I'm modeling right now. I'm modeling taking care of my body, even if it will only be for ten minutes today. Telling them it's hard, but doing it anyway.

In the shower a few minutes later, the backs of my arms shook. Out of shape never felt so good.

DAY 19

A few days ago I bought the bigs new soccer cleats. I'd considered buying myself some running shoes while we were at the store, but didn't because I didn't want to spend the money. It had been years since I'd invested in workout clothes or shoes for myself (remember, fashion sense is not my highest strength). I recognized as it was happening that I was pulling a classic mom move—taking care of everyone else's needs but not my own.

That had been bothering me, so today I went back and bought myself running shoes (okay, they were on clearance) and a hot pink water bottle. A special trip. All for me. It's okay to invest in my care with money too. Oh, it's hard for this frugal mama, but I'm making myself do it. And now drinking water is fun.

And when that self-care guilt creeps in, I remind myself that taking care of my body is not just for my benefit. It also gives those I love the best version of me I can offer.

DAY 20

8:00 p.m. Fell asleep on my bed while the rest of the house was still up and crazy.

8:30 p.m. Woke up to Derek scolding the littles for sneaking his phone to play games on it. Stumbled into their room and lay down with Lalo to help her fall asleep. I also fell back asleep in the process.

8:45 p.m. Gracie woke me up to snuggle with her. I moved to her bed.

11:45 p.m. I woke up in Gracie's bed still fully dressed. Went to my room, changed into pajamas. Lay in bed wide awake until 2:00 a.m.

No wonder I'm exhausted all the time.

DAY 21

Four days into my new DVD workout routine and the DVD gets stuck in the drive that connects to my computer. It won't play. It won't come out. I'm all dressed in the exercise uniform, leggings and a T-shirt, ready to go. And I can't get it to work.

One might think I should choose a different activity or give up, change my clothes, and move on with my day. But I am determined to work out and unable to mentally adjust. I keep going back to the computer, like the dumb rat in the science experiment, only to find it still doesn't work.

Finally, when I have a thirty-minute window between picking up Gabi and Genevieve, I do some sit-ups on the floor. There. Done. Ten minutes of abs counts!

Now I can get ready for my day. It's only 3:30, after all.

DAY 22

Today is World Water day. The World Health Organization recommends 7.1 liters of clean water for people to meet their individual drinking, cooking, and hygiene needs.

We're told 748 billion people do not have access to adequate clean water[2] and I boohoo my way to the bathroom (which by the way includes indoor plumbing, that flushes away all yuck with more clean water), thinking I'm making so many trips because of all the water I've consumed from my kitchen faucet. You know—clean, cold, tasty water.

Sometimes relishing what's right in front of me simply involves remembering what I have. That my first world problems are just that.

I fill my pink water bottle with a prayer. *Thank you, Lord, for this. I have no idea why you put me in this position, with this safe, clean water, and so much more readily available to me. Let me not take it for granted. Amen.*

DAY 23

Optometrist. Costco. Uneventful. Only took me ten years.

I make it sound easy because in a way it was. But I had to schedule on a Friday night, our only evening without a pre-planned activity and when Derek was home so I could have childcare. Something as simple as an eye appointment sometimes requires a spreadsheet's worth of maneuvering to get there.

It turns out my eyes haven't actually changed all that much in the last decade. It's all in my head. I'd like to make some snarky comment like, "I wish I could say the same about some other parts of my body," but I'll stop myself. That's not the spirit of this month's experiment.

DAY 24

I can't help but wonder how God relates to having a body. It's funny to think of Jesus having B.O. or hair that smelled from dust and sweat. To think of him clipping his fingernails and trying to scratch that itch on his back. I am not trying to be irreverent, just the opposite. I'm trying to understand his humanity. His embodiment, as we like to call it in church circles. Our bodies, which carry our souls around. Jesus had one. Fully divine and fully *human*. So his organs worked, and he had hormones and growth spurts as a child. And yet the essence of him in that body was so different than ours. Completely holy. I can't think of a better word but holy.

It gives me clarity when I consider my own body. This container for a soul. The body so temporary. The soul, the essence of me, so eternal.

DAY 25

Driving Genevieve to school this morning:

"Mom, why did you say that in a sad voice?"

"I'm not sad. I don't know."

"Are you tired?"

Laughing, I say, "I'm always tired."

I've had years of no sleep from a nursing baby or a pregnant belly. Last night? No such excuse. It was simply Netflix. So I'm cutting myself off. I can't seem to handle it in moderation. I either fall asleep while lying down with girls to put them to bed, or I manage to stay awake during the bedtime routine and Derek and I watch an episode or twenty of our latest show on Netflix. Be warned, midnight will come sooner than you think as you yell, "Just one more!"

Sleep is worth prioritizing. Always.

DAY 26

This breaking down of the body is becoming more of a reality. I can't say, "Not me, I'm too young," because my friend Rachel, a mom of preschoolers, died of cancer less than five months after her diagnosis. Because Heather's husband, Jon, who was the same age as me, collapsed at work and never woke up. They are my real-life reminders that this day may be all we have.

Sleep is worth prioritizing. Always.

A body broken. We're in the Lent season right now, preparing to remember Christ's body being broken. On Easter morning we will celebrate the resurrection, the overcoming of death that happens three days later. But first the body is broken. It's what we commemorate when we take communion, representing the flesh and the blood on the cross. It is that broken body that changed the course of history, on which our entire faith hinges.

Jesus's body, a holding spot for God himself. Walking around in skin, with bones and muscles and dirty, dusty feet. A man who, like us, had physical limitations, who needed to sleep. But unlike his disciples, he slept in the boat in the middle of the storm. Because while everyone else was freaking out about the circumstances swirling around, he was certain God was in charge.

Waking up in the middle of the night, I sense my own storm swirling around. My thoughts go straight to a writing deadline, Grandpa falling again, girls having healthy friendships, and the years that are slipping away, and what if Derek dies tomorrow just like Jon did? I cling to the boat. *Don't let it capsize. Don't let me drown.* And in the darkness I ask God, *Please, please let me know you are close. Let me know you are near.*

DAY 29

Shifting my idea of my body as something with a "should" shape to a container that needs to do good things in the world has been on the tip of my brain for a few years. This from the book *True Beauty* articulated it best for me:

> Instead of getting on the treadmill or swimming laps to impress others, attract attention, and feel confident, we exercise to strengthen our bodies to carry out the tasks God has called us to do. We do not cut back on carbs or eat more fruits and vegetables because we are worried about how we look, but rather we maintain healthy eating habits so that our bodies may function at peak performance to serve God.[3]

Here I have a body that has miraculously helped to create four other people. I can't think of a better use for it, really. It made humans! And now I need it to be able to feed and care for and comfort these people. I need it to think, and write, and understand God's message to the world and my place in it. The better I feel, the more helpful I'll be to the people I love and more effective I'll be in my short time on this planet.

What is my body for anyway?

It's here that I ask, why do I have a body in the first place? And why should I take care of it? And the best I can muster when I search for an answer is tucked in the description of the Proverbs 31 woman:

> She sets about her work vigorously; her arms are strong for her tasks. (Prov. 31:17)

It gets back to the job I am here to do in the world. The more energy I have, the better my body works, and the more effective I can be in completing my part of God's work.

DAY 31

I can't stop thinking about my body as a means to an end. Not the end goal of the perfect body for beauty's sake. But rather this question of what is my body for? Again, Tara Owens, in her book *Embracing the Body*, captures it well:

When we are continually giving over our bodies to God, not just in our heads but in our prayers and our actions, we are able to be conduits of the power of heaven and earth.[4]

This motivates me to keep pressing on. To take care of my body is more than vanity; it allows me to better push toward God's purposes in this world.

What I Learned

This month's experiment was not about whether taking care of my body would make a difference (I knew I could do better in this area), but if it was possible to find sustainable small changes that would allow me to better relish this life. So within the time and energy constraints my reality posed, I found small tweaks that indeed helped me enjoy my days. Like incorporating treats into my workouts to help make them happen: a TLC indulgence or two while on the treadmill or a strawberry in my water, even an ice cream at the end of the walk. While recognizing that sometimes it's just plain work to get started and no one is going to do that work for me.

It gets back to the job I am here to do in the world. The more energy I have, the better my body works, and the more effective I can be in completing my part of God's work.

I better recognize that the loudest gong gets my attention when I'm prioritizing my day's tasks. And my own physical care is often silent until I hit the point of collapsing. When I prioritize my care by putting doctor's appointments and exercise into my schedule, they are more likely to happen. It turns out those little people I care for don't get upset that I'm taking care of myself. They are learning from what I model.

Focusing on my health has contributed to my overall daily contentment in one major way: gratitude. I have a body that works. The miracle that is my flesh has been highlighted as I've focused more on my body's care. And that focus alone helps me appreciate the everyday activities my body allows for. I expected this month to be all about my physical well-being. It turns out my biggest change was in my head, my perspective.

When I shifted my focus from "How can I make my body look a certain way?" to "How can I use my body for God's good today?" a lot of those little things that bothered me (and the truth is, they do bother me still) were less distracting. I'll do what I can, apply sunscreen, drink water, go to bed instead of watching another episode on Netflix, and I'll be grateful for what I have, a body that pumps blood, moves, hugs, makes dinner, eats and digests that dinner. All so I can enjoy what is right in front of me.

Practices I'll Continue

Schedule exercise into my week.

Drink as much water as I do caffeinated beverages.

Make a daily mental inventory of the good things I use my body for.

Invest in a few items that make my exercise regimen more enjoyable.

Stay up-to-date on my own medical appointments.

Questions for Reflection

1. Is it difficult to make your own physical care a priority? Why or why not?

2. What gives you energy so you can more fully enjoy life today?

3. What are you most grateful your body can do for you? For God?

Words for My Actual Life

She sets about her work vigorously; her arms are strong for her tasks. (Prov. 31:17)

MONTH 5

Unleashing the Wild

Adventure

In the end, it's not the years in your life that count.
It's the life in your years.

—Abraham Lincoln

The Need

The mundane effect of ordinary life, where each day feels like a repeat of the day before, wears on me. Sometimes I'm plain bored. *Is this all there is? All there ever will be? Loading the same dishwasher with the same cups? Driving the same route in the mornings to the same schools? While listening to the same songs on the radio and wearing the same clothes I did a few days ago? Where is the variety? The excitement? Has any possibility of adventure disappeared with the drudgery of "real life"?*

What happened to the woman who could put on a backpack, grab her passport, and jump on a plane? The practical side of being a grown-up and raising kids doesn't allow for the same thrill-seeking jaunts of the past. And the truth is I'm a little afraid to do those things I used to. Even though I'm bored with routine, I'm also resistant to change. The what-ifs paralyze me. What if something bad happens? Or I fail? My risk aversion keeps me from trying new things.

Deep down I know life should still be exciting. That there is an adventurous spirit dormant inside of me. I read a Facebook update this month from author Stasi Eldredge, who wrote, "The very fact that we long for change is a sign that we are meant to have it. Our very dissatisfaction with our weaknesses and struggles reminds us that continuing to live in them is not our destiny."[1] There is something hardwired in us to want more. To be looking for more. And while we must balance that with gratitude for what is, our actual lives, we know mixing things up some, changing the elements, might help us see where we can improve and where we can be satisfied with what's right in front of us. Where God can do a new work right where we are.

The Experiment

I will do my best to do something adventurous every day. By adventurous I mean something that requires some courage. That pushes me out of my comfort zone a little, where there is an element of the unknown, even risk. I want my kids to see me modeling that bravery is not the absence of fear, but facing the fear and pushing through regardless of the doubts and unknowns.

And adventure is something that breaks up the routine. Because sometimes we are all just a bit desperate for different.

My Actual Approach

Enjoy a weeklong staycation.

Change the order or method of daily routines.

Try a new experience or food, or face a fear each week.

DAY 1

As a child I associated adventure with globetrotting. For Derek it was mountaineering. We could make drastic changes in our lives if these were still our priorities, but they're not. I'm okay that the phase we're in keeps us closer to home than it used to. But we're not dead. There must be a place in the middle. I know I can find more adventure right where I am. I need to find it within my reality, my actual life.

We are starting our month with the week of Spring Break. And we are not going anywhere exotic. For years when Nonna and Grandpa lived in Arizona, we made the Spring Break trek south, sometimes driving, sometimes flying, to swim in their pool surrounded by cactus only minutes from the Mexico border.

No, this year in full experiment fashion, the girls and I are having our first ever, all-Denver staycation. We're doing things that mess with our version of "normal" without getting on a train or a plane. Vacation is meant to be a break from the routine and that's what we're going to do, right where we are. In our actual city. (Derek doesn't get to do this staycation. Besides, he drives around Denver all day long seeing new places.)

The kick-off day was a movie (in a real movie theater, where new movies are shown) and lunch out (at a real restaurant with a waitress). Two splurges this family of six doesn't normally indulge in because everything times six is . . . well . . . expensive. Even McDonald's is overpriced when feeding that many people. I pulled out gift cards we've had for months to places we don't normally go and took my mom with us. It already felt different.

> *Bravery is not the absence of fear, but facing the fear and pushing through regardless of the doubts and unknowns.*

DAY 2

Our staycation moved downtown. Seven of us. Me and my four children, ages twelve, nine, five, and three, walking down Denver's famous 16th Street Mall with Nonna and Grandpa. I'm normally a sight with my trail of girls following after me, but add in my mother pushing her husband in a wheelchair and we spanned many decades and the width of the sidewalk.

Knowing our Spring Break tradition of swimming in the pool had been thwarted by their recent move up North, Nonna and Grandpa treated us to a stay in a hotel with a pool for the night. We ate out at downtown restaurants surrounded by street performers and out-of-towners traveling in packs with their convention lanyards around their necks. I was seeing my city as tourists do, hanging in places only they eat, staying where they stay. And I was surprised. It looked different.

I saw the homeless teenagers and young adults who have been the center of many political battles in recent years, doing what they are known for, panhandling and hanging out among the tourists. I thought of our friends at Dry Bones, whose primary mission is to walk these streets and befriend these young people. Of Derek's effort to buy a property specifically with this group in mind, to give them a warm, safe place to call home, to have people to call family. I silently prayed as I walked by, doing what I try to do with all panhandlers, make eye contact and smile. A little acknowledgment that someone standing in front of you is human tends to go a long way in offering that person dignity.

We took the free minibus down the 16th Street Mall, figuring out how to maneuver a wheelchair between all the pedestrians and on and off the bus. Grandpa won the "Most Adventurous" award by allowing us to push him over curbs and through crowds, where he was eye level with everyone else's belt buckles. He didn't complain as we navigated the bumpy streets and searched for ramps and elevators. I pictured the disabled in our city dependent on public transportation and weathering some snowy days and frigid nights. Pushing myself out of my comfort zone usually reminds me how uncomfortable many others' lives are every day and how truly comfortable mine is. Day 2 of this adventure experiment and my empathy for other people was already growing.

We ate dinner at our governor's brewery and walked through the newly remodeled Union Station, a place rich with our family's history—the spot where, as a toddler, my father-in-law met his own father for the first time when he returned from World War II. I'd visited the restored historic landmark, but had not been below with the bus tunnels and commuters bustling about. The wheelchair route took us down to this spot that I'd never had need to visit before, and I truly was impressed with my own Mile High City.

Trying something new right where I live gave me a fresh perspective on what's already around me.

DAY 4

No staycation would be complete without a marathon day with friends. We went to the MOPS meeting at our church, to Chick-fil-A for lunch with Kathy and her girls, and finally to the Denver aquarium.

And there at the aquarium was the challenge in front of me. I mean right in front of me, splashing: the stingrays. They glided around the shallow pool in circles, smooth and stealthy, not making a sound except for the flapping of their arms (not sure what they have, wings?) on the walls as they searched for the tiny fish being sold to kids and parents to feed them. There was nothing—*not one part of me*—that wanted to feed these creatures dead, cold fish from my hands. Who makes a petting zoo of stingrays, anyway? Kathy was nice and bought the girls sardines for sale to feed them. Lalo clutched her little canned fish with her pudgy paws. Looked down at her hands and then at me. We didn't have to speak to agree this wasn't the best idea.

> *Trying something new right where I live gave me a fresh perspective on what's already around me.*

Why did Kathy buy these? I thought. *What's the point? She's just more adventurous than I am. Okay, I should do this. I should model courage to my kids in this way. I can stand on a stage and speak to rooms full of people, the number one fear of Americans, right? Public speaking? Yeah, no problem. But this, no thank you.*

I was annoyed at the aquarium for having this silly touch pool and at Kathy for being fun enough to try it. The reality? I'm embarrassed that I was too scared to feed the stingrays.

DAY 5

All day my pastor Steve's words were ringing in my ears. He'd been our speaker the day before at our MOPS meeting. He made a comment in casual conversation before his talk that spoke right to me. I couldn't help but think it was meant for me in an unintentional way. He said, "I stopped trying to impress people a long time ago. I realized when I'm trying to impress someone, I'm not loving them well."

Though I'd rather not believe it, I'm most likely to take a risk, try something new, when I'm working to impress people. I'd rather love people.

DAY 6

I was invited to attend a focus group for a writing project I'm working on. The topic was women and shame. Now, that sounds like a good time, right? I was the note taker during the discussion, a neutral bystander. I listened and typed, asked a few questions, but mostly tried to hear for the feelings behind the words.

When I walked into the room, everyone in attendance was connected only to a single woman, the coordinator of the event who had invited them there. Other than that, they were total strangers to one another. A couple of people knew one other person, but mostly everybody was in the same position, that of being anonymous. And with the heavy topic at hand, the discussion could have gone two ways: people could have shared with vulnerability and depth or kept it all on the surface. Because who would know the difference?

I was floored by where the conversation quickly headed. This group chose to go the route of vulnerable, and fast. Because here is what the group had in common: they all believed God loved them. It didn't mean topics

Sometimes adventure happens when you show up to a group with your heart wide open.

weren't difficult, that embarrassment wasn't there, but they wanted to push through the lie that their choices and circumstances determined their worth.

Sometimes adventure happens when you show up to a group with your heart wide open. When you experience women looking to the Healer, the one who made them, to bind up their wounds and kiss their scars as they courageously fight forward.

In fact, that might be the truest form of adventure.

DAY 9

Routine. The perfectly executed drop-offs and pick-ups. Drive the same routes, say the same silent prayers for girls as they get out of the car. Pick them up in the same places. It was the anti-experiment day.

Some might call this boring. Today I'm choosing to call it gloriously uneventful.

DAY 10

Three girls and I had half an hour to kill in between school pick-ups. We could have stayed at the playground as usual, or been practical and stopped at the grocery store, but a little spontaneity was in order. So we played the left, right, straight game in the car. I drove a block at a time. At each intersection the girls took turns telling me "Right," "Left," or "Straight." In a city neighborhood with short blocks, this game works well.

At the end of our allotted time we found ourselves at the Broncos' stadium. Though we drive by the stadium frequently, we'd never been on many of the blocks we drove today. We saw the neighborhood that several of my daughters' classmates live in, the side of the school we don't have need to travel often because of our set routines. Where the music pouring out of the open doors had lyrics in other languages. And it offered us new eyes.

A mini-adventure to break up the monotony.

DAY 11

I've been a follower of Jesus more than half my life.

I associate lots of daily "shoulds" with that statement. At the top of that list is Bible study. I read the Bible some, and I read about the Bible a lot. I hear professionals, pastors, Bible teachers, and theologians give their take on it. But opening the Bible and asking questions, and studying meaning and context, I don't do that as often as I think I "should." So insecurities creep in.

When will I ever feel enough in this area? Probably when I have the whole thing memorized. (Please note the sarcasm here. Just to be clear, I will *never* have the whole thing memorized.)

An invitation by a group of women at church drew me in. A group of longtime friends who know me and my history, and women I didn't know well but wanted to. So despite my I'm-not-enough fears, I said yes to this weekly get-together. Because I'm working on not impressing people, but loving them. I'm working on risking.

These words from the day's study pierced straight to my core: "One of the great fears of my life is that I would get to the end of my life and realize I lived for the wrong things."[2]

What am I chasing after?

DAY 12

I approached my day with that question ringing in my ears. *What am I chasing after?* Part of me wants to make God happy, but so much of me wants to make other people happy. To impress them.

And I had two speaking engagements today. Not usual for me. For the first one, I'd prepared for months. Why? It was an audience I wanted to impress. The second was a friendlier group, or at least more familiar, so not as intimidating. I didn't spend as much time in preparation, but yes, even this room full of church ladies? I wanted to impress them.

Part of my adventure is facing my fears. And though I get nervous, I realized, it's not the speaking that makes me nervous; it's the potential for disappointing people that does. What if in my efforts to make other people happy I was living for all the wrong things?

DAY 13

I was ready for my favorite kind of day. A writing day. The kids were all arranged at schools and with the sitter. I was waiting for a call from my editor as I sat in the minivan, parked in the Starbucks parking lot, eating my breakfast sandwich. The plan was to take the call in the car and then head to the library for hours of quiet writing.

My phone rang. I looked down. Another mom from Gabi's school. I let it go to voicemail. I had only two minutes before my scheduled call. I couldn't start a conversation now. And then a text from the same mom.

> Did you hear about the lock down. For real. Kid with a gun!

My heart stopped, suspended in time as every school shooting news story swirled in my head.

Suddenly I noticed the helicopter circling overhead in the bright blue sky.

I thought I might throw up. Gabi. The middle school. I was shaking. I called the friend who texted.

"It's over," she said. "Everything's okay. It's on the news and the SWAT team is still there. But it's over."

How did she sound so calm? So confident that everything was okay? I needed to talk to Derek.

In the ten seconds it took him to answer my call, the tears had started and were full stream down my face. I couldn't take my eyes off the helicopter. There was no question it was circling the middle school only blocks away.

"I feel like I want to go get her," I said. "Just be near her."

"Go."

I was relieved my husband was so certain. Any fears of being the hysterical, dorky mom were going to have to be tabled. I tried taking deep breaths as I drove the few blocks, not knowing what I would find. I pictured men in riot gear refusing to let me in, police cars surrounding the building. As I pulled up a block away I saw police cars by the dozen, but it felt like just as many television cameras. *How many stations are there in Denver, anyway?* There were a few grandmas walking out of the school with kids, so I knew I could go in. I could go get her.

So many people. Police, all in bulletproof vests. And parents and grandparents streaming in. I wanted to cup each person's face in my hands and kiss their cheeks. These police officers who showed up for my child. These grandmas whose expressions showed they didn't understand this brave new world. I decided it wouldn't be appropriate. Besides, I was exerting all my energy in not crying. I knew my middle schooler wouldn't appreciate it.

As we walked out the front door, Derek called. "Where are you?"

"Walking out of the school. I have her."

"Oh wait. I'll call you right back," he said.

As we walked away from the building, I relaxed just enough that the tears started. Another mom, someone I'd never seen before, was walking in my direction, on her way toward the school. Seeing my tears, she reached her hand out and touched my arm as we passed. Strangers, but not. She knew exactly how I was feeling. My daughter walking next to me was perplexed, even embarrassed, by my emotions. To her the whole event had been no big deal and she thought I was just overreacting. Maybe I was, but I didn't care. I wanted her close to me the rest of the day. Where I could touch her, and hug her, and see she was okay.

I drove only a block and had to pull over. I was crying too hard. I put my head on the steering wheel and let the tears come. "Praise Jesus," I said out loud. "Praise Jesus." I've never said those words more earnestly. I was so grateful my girl and all her schoolmates were okay.

I looked down at my phone in my lap. Derek texted me a video he'd taped of us walking out of the school. The front door of the building was being streamed live on a local TV news station's website.

We went to Derek's office and out to lunch. I took her to the mall and spent way too much money. I didn't care. I just kept thinking, *What if today had turned out differently? What if?*

This was not the kind of adventure I was planning for this month, but it's the adventure life dealt me.

DAY 14

We watched the news last night. Learning what happened: two boys brought guns and a third a "smoke device." They were arrested.[3] Simply surreal to have our school the leading story. And today on the front page of the *Denver Post*, our school, where one of our children goes every day to learn, to joke with friends, and stays after to play soccer.

> *This was not the kind of adventure I was planning for this month, but it's the adventure life dealt me.*

Life still needed to happen. Two soccer games. A dinner celebration at our house for my father-in-law's birthday. That meant all the last-minute cleaning and shopping to have dinner for eight adults and ten kids ready and a house that was somewhat presentable. And the whole time I kept thinking, *What if today had turned out differently?* Just like the day Heather's husband, Jon, collapsed at work. She didn't start that Friday morning, just as I hadn't started yesterday, with the idea that life would forever change.

We celebrated Opa's birthday with cake and candles and all his kids, both by birth and marriage, and his grandkids around him. I love birthdays because they are about celebrating the fact that God made someone, not what they've accomplished or will get done, but that they simply are. And they come around no matter the circumstances. I wouldn't have scheduled this dinner party amid the stress and chaos of the day before. I was emotionally exhausted, but it was there and we still needed to—in fact, more than ever wanted to—celebrate God's goodness in the eye of the storm.

I'm grateful for marker days, holidays, birthdays, anniversaries that remind us to not let the difficult overcome the good.

> *I'm grateful for marker days, holidays, birthdays, anniversaries that remind us to not let the difficult overcome the good.*

DAY 15

We've been studying the Psalms at church, those songs David wrote with an earnest heart amid all of his bad choices. Today was Psalm 23, probably the most famous of them all.

> The LORD is my shepherd, I lack nothing.
>> He makes me lie down in green pastures,
> he leads me beside quiet waters,
>> he refreshes my soul.
> He guides me along the right paths
>> for his name's sake.
> Even though I walk
>> through the darkest valley,
> I will fear no evil,
>> for you are with me;
> your rod and your staff,
>> they comfort me.[4]

Unlike David, I couldn't say I wouldn't have fear. Everything felt unsure. Fear felt close and thick. How could my worst nightmare, that thing I couldn't even utter out loud, guns at my child's school, actually happen? If facing fear was adventure, I certainly was see-ing adventure. I could use it to grow closer to God or farther from him. My prayer: *Lord, help me in this dark valley.*

DAY 16

The girls had a school day off. A Monday for hanging around, and one more day before I had to take Gabi back to the front steps that were all over the news and drop her off.

We went to the park. Always one to multitask, I took work with me.

"Mom, will you shoot baskets with me?" Genevieve asked. I knew she must be desperate for a playmate if she was asking the least sporty of the family to join her in basketball. I looked down at my books and papers that I'd lugged the three blocks to the park, and said, "Yes."

DAY 17

This is what courage looks like. I pulled up to Gabi's school as I did every day, a mass of cars and kids and parents, many of the latter headed to work. And just like every day she got out of the car with her backpack, turned her back toward me, and walked toward the swarm of short boys and tall girls that make up middle school. But of course today felt different. As I watched her walk away, part of my heart went right there along with her as though it were tucked in her backpack attached to her. I said the same prayer I've said so many other days: "Lord, please, *please,* protect her." And I drove away.

At home, I was surprised to read our Bible study passage today. Psalm 23. Just like Sunday's sermon.

> He guides me along the right paths
>   for his name's sake. (NIV)

Do I trust him to guide me? To do right by me? By my family? For his purposes? Answering yes to that feels like an adventure.

DAY 18

The littles and I packed into the car for a morning drive in the mountains. I was speaking at a MOPS group about an hour west of Denver, an adventure for me as I looked at the map and the mountain roads and trusted my phone would direct us there. Thinking through our day's schedule, I decided enjoying the drive both up and down the mountain was more important than preschool, so Gracie would be skipping her morning class, allowing us to linger in the mountains as long as we liked.

Once off the highway, as we were winding through smaller roads, my backseat city girls noticed things looked a little different, unusual. With every turn there was a new discovery. A meadow. Horses. A stream. Nothing out of the ordinary for the kids they would be joining at MOPS who call these roads home. But for my girls the "oohs" and "aahs" were plenty. (The over-acting indicated they've maybe watched a few too many episodes from the Disney Channel.) Our little trek was offering us all a new adventure.

One of the MOPS moms suggested we visit the elk preserve next to the church after the meeting. I drove the minivan along the dirt road between the church and a barn, and though the elk were asleep and not engaging with us in the slightest, we did discover that the barn had been converted into a chapel. A place for weddings, it looked like.

"Can we go in?" Gracie asked as we stood at the front door. The pickup parked in the driveway indicated someone was around, so I put my hand on the chapel's door handle and turned it. We walked inside and all three of our heads moved in unison to look up to the rafters, two stories above us. The strings of lights crisscrossing each other hinted at parties waiting to happen. It felt like a big person's fairyland.

"This is a special place," I told the girls in almost a whisper as we walked out the door. Sometimes adventure is a simple trek off the usual road.

DAY 20

In studying adventure this month, I learned there is a classic experiment about maximizing change-related stress. In 1908 two famous British psychologists discovered there is an "optimal anxiety," a low-level stress that helps people perform better. But there is a tipping point; once you pass the optimal stress level you become much less productive. Breaking up routines can help you mix things up enough to raise anxiety to that optimal point. Crises are just too much and have the opposite effect because they cross the tipping point and make us less productive.[5]

Sometimes adventure is a simple trek off the usual road.

I'm still too shaken to get anything done. I guess adventure in moderation is what's going to help me love my actual life.

DAY 22

Derek and I tend to do our own things work-wise. I support him at home, make sure he has clean socks to wear, and do my best to listen attentively, but I don't get involved in the day-to-day events of Prov.

But then a graduate of Prov, Spencer, decided to go on a trip—a very long bike trip from San Francisco to New York. He wanted to raise awareness about young adults and addictions and homelessness. That is his story. He was in his early twenties when he came to Prov. He has a direct connection to the new home's mission, and he wants to help raise money by riding his bike from the Golden Gate Bridge to the Brooklyn Bridge. Who *does* that?!

Lord knows I can't ride that bike with him, but I can support him. I can join the adventure from here. I spent the day calling television stations and tweeting reporters I know to see if I could help him get the word out on this end. Not at all a typical day for me, but this I can do.

Do what only you can do.

DAY 24

I had an urgency that Spencer's story was worth telling. For this is what God was showing me. This! This work, his work, is what's worth telling. I can edit. I can wordsmith. I can give my gifts to the larger mission. Derek can figure out how to make this home happen. I can email reporters.

DAY 25

I woke up excited to join some of Derek's team at a meeting about the capital campaign for the building. Nothing glamorous, just some staff and volunteers committed to raising money to make this new house happen. Sitting around a long coffee shop table, sometimes everyone talking at once. I could tell we all felt part of something. That God is working and we not only get to witness it, but we get to have a part in making it happen.

There was the practical side of me getting to the meeting. I had to arrange for a babysitter, reschedule my turn to help in the preschool classroom, drive halfway across town. But it was palpable that this is God's work. If that's not worth a little rearranging, I'm not sure what is.

DAY 26

I could hardly catch my breath today. So many things on my to-do list felt urgent, but so many of them felt like holy duties. Emails. Phone calls. Articles. Much was writing related, but much was Spencer related. Helping Derek with some edits. I thought of the quote I'd heard once, "Hit the floor each day so that Satan says, 'Oh ****! She's awake!'" I've rarely lived with that kind of urgency, that God's work has propelled me forward with such clarity of purpose.

I've felt in the right space before, but this was a new feeling. I suspect it's because I've seen what God is doing with this new house project, the miraculous details that shout redemption from every space, and I've wanted to join him. Rather than asking God to bless the plans I've made—because I always have some kind of agenda ready to hand over to the Maker of the universe—I was seeing God's plan and how I can contribute in my small way.

> Rather than asking God to bless the plans I've made . . . I was seeing God's plan and how I can contribute in my small way.

DAY 27

At the last minute, I was given a ticket to a conference happening in town. A bunch of churchy types talking storytelling. I could almost melt—it's my favorite kind of thing, listening to good communicators communicate about how to best communicate the good news. That message that Jesus is real and for us. Speaker after speaker stood up and talked through the parables, explaining how Jesus answered questions with stories that made no sense. When a doubter or follower asked Jesus a question, he would often answer with a story that didn't seem connected with the question being asked. That left people puzzled. This is how the one who knew everything, who had all the answers, chose to communicate.

I love that Jesus doesn't package things in neat, bullet point statements. He leaves the gray for us to muddle through. (Wait, I guess I only like that sometimes.) But it helps to know that even the people who were able to touch Jesus and talk to him face-to-face were confused a lot of the time. In this journey of figuring out what the heck we are here for, it helps to know most of us are more than a bit confused as we stumble through our adventures.

DAY 28

Sometimes plans change. That's part of the adventure, right? Making adjustments. I had my day figured out. Nice and neat to meet my needs, and I liked the plan very much.

A Saturday in April with no scheduled soccer games. Miracles still happen. I'd coordinated with Derek so I could get some work done and then go off to a hair appointment. I never, I mean never, get a whole Saturday to delve into work. It was a treat of a day. But Grandpa wasn't feeling well and Nonna had tickets to a play, so I rescheduled my hair appointment and went to their house so he wouldn't be alone while she took Gracie to the play.

> *The best adventures are the ones God is already doing and we simply join him.*

If the adventure is greatest when I watch what God is doing and join in, I must also be obedient in the non-epic moments. And recognize God is here in the quiet obedience of sitting with someone. To not see our changed plans as a burden, something to grouch about, but another opportunity for adventure. Because where God is, adventure is. And he is everywhere.

Because truly I want to savor the moments I have with this man. Sitting with him was a gift offered. I will not get today back. So yes, changed plans, I will not try to control you. I will graciously say yes to you and see what God might have for me in my actual day.

DAY 30

We said good-bye to Spencer tonight. We went to Providence House, where he lived for two years while he learned to maneuver life sober. We circled around him and prayed and then ate cake.

I felt so proud of this young man and grateful to be part of Prov's newest property. For three years, Spencer has planned this ride, and I'm just jumping on the bandwagon at the end. I'm honored to be part of someone's steadfastness and dedication to something bigger than himself. The best adventures are the ones God is already doing and we simply join him.

What I Learned

There is a time to get out of a rut and try something new. Breaking up the established routine reminds me that I can keep growing, learning, and changing. And it helps me see the familiar with new eyes, helps me appreciate all the good right in front of me that goes unnoticed.

And then there's recognizing that the normal everyday is pretty good, even pretty amazing. This month helped me remember that wishing for more excitement isn't necessarily the goal. Because excitement can in fact be more difficult than the humdrum of regular life. It can come in the form of crisis. Sometimes today's slow and quiet or chaotic and loud—whatever my current version of normal pace may be—is better than the alternative.

I will not get today back.

I also experienced a sense of adventure that isn't about impressing others, but about following what God is doing right here, in my own little circle of influence. My neighborhood, my children's schools, my family. And that my "little" gestures can contribute to a larger picture than I might ever see. I have opportunities every day to embrace working with God rather than working my own plan. I don't need to go far to look for adventure. The best kind is right where he is. My job is to notice what he's doing so I can do my part to make it happen. What could be more exciting than that?

Practices I'll Continue

Explore my city.

Celebrate established, marker holidays.

Mix up daily routines.

Work on loving people over impressing them.

Watch for what God is already doing and join him in it.

Questions for Reflection

1. What area of your life feels mundane? How can you mix it up?
2. Does the idea of adventure make you nervous or excited? Why?
3. How can you join what God is already doing?

Words for My Actual Life

He guides me along the right paths for his name's sake. (Ps. 23:3)

MONTH 6

Pushing Through the Piles

Home Organization

Home is the nicest word there is.

—Laura Ingalls Wilder

The Need

My lack of home organization creates more stress than I'd like. I'm late because I had to spend ten minutes looking for my car keys. My children don't know what to wear because the clean and dirty piles in the laundry room have melded into one huge Mt. Everest and it's time to leave for school *now!* A friend texts to say she's on her way to drop off a pan I left at her house. I'm more panicked about her seeing the current state of my kitchen than I am excited to see this precious person who is about to pull into my driveway.

Science shows our environments play a role in our stress levels. Everyday elements from lighting to noise can impact us in negative ways.[1] Details like a hot room or a burned-out lightbulb can seem minor in life's big stressor scheme, but can unknowingly grate on us. When I experience the compounded stress of walking into the same messy room multiple times in a given day, it has a cumulative effect.

I spend more time, energy, and attention on doing double the work when systems are not in place to keep my busy life in order. And I'm not able to fully give people the warm welcome I'd like when I'm scrambling to get the house organized. Stopping long enough to make a few intentional changes takes discipline, but will free up my time and attention so I can offer them to the parts of my life I most value—the people. I've always placed my value on people over possessions, but what if my possessions require a little attention so I can better tend to the people?

The Experiment

I will make small tweaks in my home and its management to create a higher sense of order and peace for those who are inside it.

My Actual Approach

Organize two rooms in my home over the month.

Spend at least thirty minutes daily organizing or cleaning.

Invite friends over once a week.

DAY 1

Let's just get this out from the get-go; part of the problem here is me. I'm not organized by nature. I can step over toys when walking through a room and, well, just keep walking.

I get overwhelmed, paralyzed really, with this kind of experiment because it feels like hurtling into a black hole of LEGOs and mismatched socks. If there is any experiment that can offer me real, practical, needed help, it's this one. But I have to be pushed here because, Lord knows (and he truly does because he witnesses it daily), I let a lot of things slide in this area.

So what's going to motivate me? I've been writing and doing life long enough to know what gets me to take action: deadlines. I'm a procrastinator and an easily distractinator (this must be a word). And I'm great at starting projects and not so great at finishing them. So deadlines are key for me. And they can't be self-imposed either, because, well, those aren't really deadlines. Who are we kidding?

My friend Ashley is coming to visit us in a few days. Overnight. In our guest room. The room also known as the wrapping paper, old vase, MOPS craft supplies, storage room.

It needs a makeover in a big way. The blankets don't quite fit the queen-sized bed. The bed is currently covered in toys, glitter, wrapping paper, and even a piece of chewed-up gum. A vacuum cleaner and broken shelving set sit next to the bed. Nothing about this room feels like a welcoming spot for a living creature. This is my first project. I will go with the deadline—Ashley's arrival. May it dictate my actions.

So today I started with some pictures I was planning to have framed for my office. Why would I start with an office project when the room at hand is the guest bedroom? Because that's how house projects work, right? I start with one, but that means I need to go back to another. I have managed to collect enough pictures, frames, and artwork for ten rooms, all under the guise that they're "for the office." There certainly must be some for the guest bedroom in that pile. I look through all of it, and I frame some photos. Something I've been meaning to do for a year. And they look beautiful. None of them will go in the guest bedroom, but they look lovely and I am quite pleased with myself.

DAY 2

We got the call: the rain canceled all soccer games for the day. So with hours of unexpected free time and our car already en route to the southern Denver suburbs, we made a detour to IKEA. The littles walked into an hour of free childcare, happy to jump into the germ-laden ball pit, and I went off to scope out the bedding for the guest bedroom. In one hour: maze of IKEA maneuvered, bedding purchased, one guest bedroom about to be redone.

A second stop at Target that evening for a few accent pillows and curtains and we were golden.

Sometimes it's just makin' it hap'n, cap'n.

DAY 3

Well, isn't this perfect? I was so impressed with myself the last two days, and not one thing was organized today. Not one. Unless of course you count driving to soccer practice, three school drop-offs and pick-ups, one ballet lesson, and making dinner for six.

Then yes, my regular Monday feels like an organizational coup! I'm going to let the administration of people count today. They reside in our home and need to be moved around, right?

I'm pushing the borders of the experiment a little early in this month's game, but I have to work within my reality, which is that this home organization/simplification thing is just not my bent.

DAY 4

Ashley will be here in two days. The purchases for the guest bedroom remodel are waiting outside the room's door because there isn't enough space on the other side to allow them in. But here's the benefit of being a procrastinator: sometimes it helps me get tons done, just not in the desired area. In my attempts to avoid getting the guest room ready I organized the books spread over my office floor, unpacked boxes from the move from my working-outside-the-home office months earlier, and cleaned out the laundry room. So many organizational victories in the midst of procrastination.

DAY 5

I suffer from moving pile syndrome: Where I move piles of papers from one place on the kitchen counter to another. Where I move piles of clean laundry from one room of the house to another. Where I move piles of cleats and socks and toys from the car into my house and plop them wherever they seem to find themselves.

Touch everything once. That's the principle as I clean up my house for our guest. I've heard this before and it was recently reiterated. Touch everything once, meaning don't simply move something to the room where it belongs if you can put it all the way away. Another way of looking at it is if it takes less than two minutes to do, do it.

Washing out the sink? Hanging up the coats? If I see a task that needs to be done and I can complete said task in less than 120

Touch everything once.

seconds, I do it. And if I'm putting laundry "away," that means more than leaving it folded on top of the dryer. And more than delivering said laundry to various bedrooms (common symptoms of moving pile syndrome). It is taking it and putting it . . . All. The. Way. Away.

DAY 6

In true procrastinator fashion, I cleaned up to the last available minute before rushing out the door to go to the airport. As I grabbed my purse off its designated hook in the mudroom, I saw the vacuum cleaner stationed at the bottom of the stairs, right smack where Ashley would be walking to get to her new, pretty guest quarters.

> *The key is preparing my house so others feel welcome to come and spend time.*

All this work to get the curtains up and pictures hung and I left the vacuum right in the middle of the walkway. I didn't have time to figure out where it should go now that I could no longer store it in the guestroom, and I walked out the door.

But here's the thing. Ashley is my friend. Yes, she has never seen my house before and I want it to feel welcoming and not disgusting. But she is coming to see *me* and my family. There is a point to letting the perfection go (which I seem to have no problem with, which brings us to this problem in the first place). The key is preparing my house so others feel welcome to come and spend time.

And because the room was a little prettier, I was happy to show Ashley to her space (and I told her not to look in the closet).

DAY 7

I learned a new word this week: *floordrobe*. I immediately understood its meaning because my bedroom closet is a full-fledged floordrobe. But for those who may not be as familiar with the word, it means your floor acts as a wardrobe. I have the luxury of having my own closet. Unlike any other space in our house, I don't share it with anyone. I share my bed, my toilet, and my office with at least one other person. Anywhere else in my home, I clean, organize, tidy, decorate with someone almost always right behind me undoing what's been done. But my closet is really my own little corner of the world.

It's not a walk-in; more like a stand-in. It is possible to play hide-and-seek and close the door behind you without being smothered in the closet. That is, if the floordrobe isn't in effect.

With half an hour in my Saturday afternoon to use for organizing purposes, I stood facing my floordrobe and thought, *I'll just hang things back up and in half an hour I'll have a cleaner closet.* Oh the naiveté of someone who should know that organizing after months of procrastinating takes time.

I worked for half an hour hanging up clothes, finding lost earrings, putting away shoes. But then Derek walked by on his way back out to the garage—where I'd heard the power tools of my tinkerer-husband—for some Mother's Day gift making. So I stopped him as he walked through the room and asked him to hang the necklace holder Genevieve had made for me months ago: a piece of scrap wood found in the garage with dabs of pink paint making a polka-dot pattern, and two rows of nails acting as hooks pounded into it. Then I refolded my sweaters and stacked them on the shelf above my hanging clothes.

I kept at it. Half an hour turned into an hour, into two. And my usual, stop-halfway-into-a-project self kept going. Then with everything tucked away into its proper spot, I sat on the edge of the bed and looked at my closet, doors open, displaying all the contents.

Derek walked by again.

"What are you looking at?"

"There's just so much of it."

Always wanting me to purge, he said, "How about you try to get rid of half of it?"

"I'm overwhelmed."

There certainly was a new sense of order, but something about the order emphasized the volume. Maybe I will get rid of some, but for now I need to stop. This unorganized woman needs to allow these two hours of organizing to be a victory.

DAY 8

I woke up to a Mother's Day breakfast in bed. Frozen waffle toasted, with smears of butter, peanut butter, and jam. All on our family's red plate with the words "You Are Special" etched around the outer rim. Chocolate milk in a champagne flute and homemade cards. I sat and soaked it in. A year with all my girls still at home, waking up in their beds and running to jump into mine. The overfull cup of coffee ready to spill at every wiggle of little tushies snuggled in next to mine. I'm aware that the years of Mother's Days with this as the scene are numbered. I willed myself to put it into my brain and remember. So many parts of my life feel unremembered already—baby moments I was sure would never leave the recall, gone.

I got out of bed, carrying my breakfast tray, and walked by my closet. The clean floor caught my eye and I stopped, turned, and admired the beautiful space. I could almost hear the chorus of angels singing their hallelujah in unison and see the heaven-like scene of sunrays shooting between clouds toward my vanished floordrobe. It was a Mother's Day gift I gave myself. How does one little piece of organized space give me such joy? Perhaps control in a life that feels out of control? Or simply all the rediscovered clothes and jewelry that hadn't been visible in the disaster zone? I wasn't sure, but I was more excited to get dressed than I had been in a long time.

DAY 9

God has organized his creation in some pretty amazing ways. I think of the water cycle, human organs, the solar system—all structures that make the world work. So why is it that I can't seem to find one system for keeping trash out of the car?! (I will consider my car an extension of my home for this experiment's purposes. I spend enough time there.)

I'm realizing part of the issue is I'm doing the work of six people (well, five really, because Derek's pretty good about putting his laundry away). There's a certain element of home organization every mom must tackle: teaching her children to be (somewhat) self-sufficient. We are working on this principle: If you bring it into the car you must take it out of the car when we return home. If you bring it into the house, you do not dump it on the mudroom floor as soon as you step over the garage door's threshold.

> Train up a child in the way he should go;
>   even when he is old he will not depart from it.
>   (Prov. 22:6 ESV)

I'm not sure God had keeping my car clean in mind when these words were written to instruct parents for thousands of years on how to raise their children. But right now the way they should go is toward the trash can in the garage and the shoe bin in the mudroom. With their stuff in their hands.

DAY 10

I was at Target today in the office supply section and felt the need to buy stuff to help me get more organized. With entire stores, industries, and professionals dedicated to home organization, I could spend some serious money in this realm. But more importantly, there must be something out there I can buy that will help me, right? Some "thing" that will help me figure out what I need to make it all work. So I bought the biggest item in the office supply aisle because my needs are big and I figure size indicates effectiveness. I bought a wall calendar with sticky notes and task management spaces. A grid for all of what, I'm not sure. But it looked official. It looked like it could help me.

DAY 11

The pick-up-as-I go-method, that's what I'm trying today. Pick something up as I walk through a room and put it in its proper place as I pass through other rooms or even take a detour. It's a constant moving of stuff. But I'm walking through the house anyway, so I might as well be putting things away.

DAY 12

As I walked on the treadmill this evening, I watched the news on ABC and they highlighted a graduation speech that went viral the year before. Naval Admiral William H. McRaven at the University of Texas said, "If you want to change the world, start off by making your bed."[2] His emphasis was on excellence in the little things. It struck me as true. If I want to do big things for good, I must focus on the small tasks in front of me. Do them with excellence. So that I am freed up to do the monumental. And, really, all big tasks are made up of many little ones.

> If you make your bed every morning you will have accomplished the first task of the day. It will give you a small sense of pride and it will encourage you to do another task and another and another. By the end of the day, that one task completed will have turned into many tasks completed. Making your bed will also reinforce the fact that little things in life matter.
>
> If you can't do the little things right, you will never do the big things right.
>
> And if by chance you have a miserable day, you will come home to a bed that is made—that you made—and a made bed gives you encouragement that tomorrow will be better.
>
> If you want to change the world, start off by making your bed.[3]

I knew it. I knew making your bed was more than just making your bed.

DAY 13

The laundry room with its brown plaid wallpaper and faux wood cabinets has been a mess for days. Days. And it's almost entirely clean clothes that need to be folded and put away. They are strewn everywhere. In and out of baskets, on top of the washer and dryer, and of course on the floor in piles. I'm sick of it and yet nothing has motivated me to jump in and tackle the mountain. Enter that familiar feeling of being overwhelmed with where to begin. If only people were coming over, the risk of them seeing this mess would motivate me to do something about it.

> *If I want to do big things for good, I must focus on the small tasks in front of me.*

And then the brilliant idea. I have a whole bunch of people right at my fingertips. I got my phone, snapped a picture of the chaos, and posted it on Instagram, Twitter, and Facebook with this caption: *This is my laundry room in all of its 1970s messy glory. It's looked like this for days and I'm tired of it. So to keep myself from procrastinating anymore I am sharing with the promise I will post when it is clean. Building in motivation by capitalizing on public self-outing here. #LovingMyActualLife*

And you know what the response was?

"Thank you for sharing! It really does help to see that I'm not alone in the 'mess' lol."

"This just made my day! Thanks! I feel so liberated!!"

"Best. post. all. day.!!!!"

Some people posted photos of their own laundry rooms in the comments. It was one big internet sigh of relief that we're not alone. What started as an impulsive photo to get my butt moving ended up offering others a dose of mess they could relate to.

DAY 14

With four soccer games over the next two days, we had a divide-and-conquer approach for the weekend. You go here, and you here, and we'll decide on the littles based on if there is a playground at a given field or known younger sibling playmates on a given team.

And then Derek got a call. Saturday morning work calls are not unusual, though he does try to take weekends off. It simply isn't in the job description to not take calls when they come. I could tell from his softer tone and his chosen words that this wasn't a call with good news. I thought of Linda and wondered if she'd taken a turn for the worse. I wiped the kitchen counters as I listened to his end of the conversation. He asked questions about next steps and still I didn't know what had happened.

He hung up. A suicide in one of the Prov homes. He walked from the kitchen into our bedroom, and I followed behind, reassuring him as he got dressed that I had the day covered. And like that, our masterfully scheduled Saturday plans were turned upside down.

> *No amount of organizing prepares us for life's unexpected moments.*

No amount of organizing prepares us for life's unexpected moments. This is where flexibility comes in.

There was no question Derek needed to deal with the crisis. To go. Talk to the police. Check on the staff. And I needed to pray and get kids to soccer games. And cry for a hurting world and a Prov home turned upside down.

DAY 16

I was at Bible study today, and as we went around the table, coffee cups in one hand, tissues in the other, sharing how our weeks were going, I heard a need expressed. Not one that was explicit; no one was asking outright for help. But I heard a need and I knew I could offer something.

"Does she need a place to stay?" I asked. "She can stay in our guest room for the week."

I pictured the new duvet cover and yellow curtains and thought this might be just the refuge for a young woman coming to Denver in a few weeks. I was better prepared to offer, more quick with my words, because I knew the space was ready and waiting right now. I guess that's what having a house in order is about, the ability to easily and freely use it to meet others' needs.

DAY 17

Other than our newly redecorated guest bedroom, our house is an absolute disaster. Dis. As. Ter. Why? Because we are smack-dab in the most difficult month of the year for moms everywhere: May. (Okay, well, at least for moms in the United States. Maybe mothers in the Southern Hemisphere aren't bombarded with end-of-the-year parties ad infinitum.) And May brings Mother's Day, a birthday in our house, soccer tryouts (because we want to get a head start on next year's crazy), end-of-season parties, and tournaments.

Eleven soccer games this week. And I only have two children playing! It is the perfect storm of those make-up games, already-scheduled games, one girl in a tournament, and middle school playoffs, where Gabi's team is going all the way! Those all add up to eleven games. So guess what I am doing. Driving. Guess what I am not doing. Dishes, laundry, picking up toys and clothes.

That's what having a house in order is about, the ability to easily and freely use it to meet others' needs.

I came home from the third soccer game of the week welcomed by crusted dishes overflowing out of the sink and spreading across the counters, and thought, *The kitchen. If I just clean the kitchen it will be better.* It's the first room in the house we see as we walk through the mudroom. It's our greeting space, our "Welcome home."

Just like with the closet, I'll give myself half an hour to unload and load the dishwasher, clear the counters and wipe them down.

An hour later and things were looking better. I knew Derek could come home and not be too negatively impacted by the environment he was walking into. However, Admiral McRaven would not be pleased by the bed situation in our house. At. All.

Today I do what only I can.

Of course. Of course this week, with all the games, we scheduled a birthday party. And not a two-hour celebration but a ten-year-old slumber party! She only turns ten once, so I want to make it special, but not in the week of house disaster and driving from one game to the next to the next to the next. Any other week but this one would be better, more convenient.

As I wiped the morning's crumbs off the kitchen counter and felt the tension in my neck and shoulders increase at the thought of having to clean our house from top to bottom in the next day, I remembered my friend Francie's words a few days earlier. We were talking on the phone about our Mother's Day. Francie said she'd spent the afternoon cleaning because they were hosting a friend, a man, at their house for a retreat. Also a mother of four, with even younger kids than mine, she laughed at the thought of her house being retreat material. No quiet. But she said the last year her prayer has been that the Holy Spirit host their guests. Praying as she vacuumed her basement on Mother's Day, she again asked the Holy Spirit to be the palpable essence in their home rather than the Play-Doh and the crying.

So as I wiped, I prayed for Genevieve and her friends. That the Holy Spirit would welcome them and they would feel God's gentleness, regardless of their ability to recognize it and name it as such. That the evening would be a good, welcoming, restoring, and holy experience for these nine- and ten-year-old girls. That an air of celebration would permeate the house, because a birthday is a celebration of life and because they are all precious lives.

I felt the tightening in my chest loosen as I wiped and prayed. This wasn't about having the perfectly put-together home; it was about having a fun time, and who better to set the tone for fun than the Holy Spirit, who is in the midst of all things good?

And then I got the text from Derek about our friend who had been sick.

Linda died this morning.

DAY 20

Walking on the treadmill in the garage, the hum roaring louder than a machine should, I turned on a podcast: "This Is Your Life" with Michael Hyatt. I chose this episode because of the title, "The Disciplined Pursuit of Less." Yes! Exactly what I'm working on, right? And a few minutes into the conversation, what did the guest start talking about? Closets! That our lives are like our closets. If we don't intentionally clean them out and organize them, they become overstuffed with things we don't need.

I stopped the treadmill, walked into the house to my computer, and ordered the guest's book: *Essentialism: The Disciplined Pursuit of Less.* And when it came three days later, this is what I found:

In the same way that our closets get cluttered as clothes we never wear accumulate, so do our lives get cluttered as well-intended commitments and activities we've said yes to pile up. Most of these efforts didn't come with an expiration date. Unless we have a system for purging them, once adopted, they live on in perpetuity.[4]

Well, there you go. Cleaning out my closet was a symbolic effort in cleaning out my life. A representation of this larger experiment.

Space to breathe! Decluttering offers us that space. I'm terrible at it because I'm terrible at throwing things away. Perhaps it's the frugal side of me that thinks, *What if I need this someday? Okay, so I haven't used that picnic basket in the last eight years, but what if I need it* this *summer?* Perhaps I need a new strategy for getting rid of things. To saying no to things.

DAY 22

Did I mention it's May?

As a result, the house has thrown up on itself. I walk in, microwave whatever I can scrounge from the freezer, add the dirty dishes to the pile already in the sink, and pick through the mountain of clean clothes in the laundry room for a top and a bottom for each child to wear. We are in survival mode and everything in our home screams that.

It's moments like these when the anger starts to simmer. *Am I the only one who notices the dirty socks under the dining room table? Who feels the urge to wash the dishes? Because the truth is, there is no urge to do dishes on my part either, people! Just wanting it to get done!* I begin to feel like I'm being taken for granted.

And then I pick up some cleats from the kitchen floor and think, *It's messy because people live here.* We live here, so it's not going to look like a magazine photo spread. And people live here and they won't always. There will come a time when I'll put something down and it will still be there the next time I enter the room because I'll be all alone in the house. It makes me love the mess a little more. Appreciate it, at least. They still need to help, but a perspective change on my part never hurts.

> *It's messy because people live here.*

DAY 23

"Girls, it's time to pick up."

Twice a month I scramble around the house picking up toys, folding laundry, and dealing with the piles of papers on the kitchen counters. Are guests coming? No, two women, whom I am always delighted to see, arrive to mop my floors and clean my bathtub.

Two years ago when Derek and I were away on an anniversary trip (two nights without kids, the first time in five years, unless you count going to the hospital to have a baby, but then I guess that involves a kid), what did we talk about? (Or should I say fight about?) The constant disarray and disorganization of our home. We decided then we'd pay to have someone come clean every other week for the summer and evaluate at the end of the three months if it helped. Well, that was two years ago and they're still coming.

But the truth is, the clean these women create gets messy pretty quickly, say within two hours of everyone being home. But here is what I've found in the last few years: this every-other-week schedule of two angels showing up pushes me to keep things in order. If I want them to mop my floors, the floors can't have toys or clothes or books all over them. If I want the top of the washer and dryer to be wiped down, there can't be clothes piled to the ceiling. It's an accountability built into my month. It's okay for me to recruit help in this putting away too.

I'm cheap. I think that's been established. But I refuse to feel guilty about spending my little extra cash this way. There was a time when this splurge was too far out of budget, but these days my spare dollars don't go to lunches out or getting my nails done; they go to two women who vacuum and leave lines in my carpet in a very special way.

DAY 24

Do the next thing, right? Pick up the living room, and then tackle the kitchen. Focusing on what's right in front of me rather than picturing the entire house helps the job at hand feel more manageable.

We came home from Costco today with a minivan's worth of paper towels and bagels. As I unloaded the car and began to organize, I realized my perception of our freezer's size while standing in the frozen food aisle of Costco and its actual size were different. So I began to unpack the freezer to make room, and in the process began to throw things out that were no longer edible. Although I want to save *everything*, there comes a time when two lonely chicken nuggets with freezer burn need to be tossed. And in the process I discovered both an ice cream sandwich and a Popsicle had melted in one of the drawers, causing one giant, sticky, purple mess. Since I can't remember the last time I bought ice cream sandwiches, I'm afraid it's been that way for a long time. Twenty minutes, that's all it took, to toss and scrub and reorganize the freezer. And I want to jump up and down, I'm so happy. If this is simply resolving a first world pain, a clean freezer that can now hold all my food, I get that. But it's the little stressors that add up.

DAY 25

My friend Jennifer is an organizer. I walk into her house and automatically feel guilty. Because depending on her current foster care situation, she usually has one to three more children living in her house than I do and yet her home is immaculate. I'm constantly flabbergasted at how she pulls it off.

This morning at our weekly Bible study she showed me her summer planning chart for her children. Yes, she had a spreadsheet, and yes, it was uploaded to her phone. Her home is run the same way. But we've also had discussions around organizing. Do we manage our homes or do they manage us? Do we manage our lives or do they manage us? What's the purpose anyway? While I struggle to get a handle on my home, she struggles to loosen her grip of control.

I need to recognize that although home organization is my self-perceived weak spot, my home, like Jen's, still offers a beautiful space for our family. Room for us to be together and to always invite more in. It's not a showroom, but it's ours.

DAY 28

Derek and I went to Linda's funeral. Pews full of familiar faces, current and former staff and residents of Prov, but that was only a fraction of who was there. Linda loved people wherever she went. And as her sister stood in front of this group and spoke of Linda's generous spirit, she shared a note in Linda's handwriting she'd found earlier that week as she was going through her apartment. It said, "Philosophy of Ministry: Ministry is whoever is at the door or on the phone." And that was Linda, carrying her mobile hospitality with her. I pictured her opening her apartment door at Victory Apartments and showing whoever was standing on the other side her genuine enthusiasm. She did not have a fancy home; it was a small, two-bedroom apartment in a neighborhood that made many nervous to visit. It was her welcoming spirit and willingness to leave the door open a crack that made her home a haven for so many.

> *Do we manage our homes or do they manage us? Do we manage our lives or do they manage us?*

And then at the end of her handwritten philosophy, a footnote: "Err on the side of grace." Yes, people create messes in our homes. They are loud and certainly not convenient. But err on the side of grace.

DAY 29

Thinking about Linda's decisions, the ones she made day after day, Jesus's words reverberated in my heart:

> For I was hungry and you gave me something to eat, I was thirsty and you gave me something to drink, I was a stranger and you invited me in, I needed clothes and you clothed me, I was sick and you looked after me, I was in prison and you came to visit me.[5]

I could see Linda in his words. But could I see myself?

Lord Jesus, help me to live into your words. Amen.

DAY 30

We have family coming this weekend. They are flying standby so we aren't sure what time, even what day, they might arrive. Maybe Thursday night, maybe Friday morning. And guess what? I'm not panicked because the guest room is ready for their arrival. Well, look at that, fancy pants!

What I Learned

Though home organization intimidated me, even paralyzed me, in a way the other experiments haven't, ignoring the need for it does not get things done. So I tried a variety of approaches that worked, including putting things away as I moved from room to room, setting a timer for a concentrated organizing time, and tackling one small project with deadlines that included other people coming over. I focused on following through to the end of a project, which means I tackled less but accomplished more.

Then there's the help factor. Asking my kids to pitch in teaches them responsibility (a little bit my job, after all). And paying someone to help in this arena is okay. It just is. I don't need to be embarrassed (though truth is, I am a little because it implies I'm not capable), but for me it is admitting I'm not good at everything, especially this.

And there's the concept of stewarding, taking care of the things that have been given to me. As I try to steward my days, this collection of 24-hour periods, I also need to recognize that my things and the place I spend much of my time also need to be well cared for. Because the more they are prepared for the potential guest, the more freely I swing the door open when someone is actually on my doorstep. This is not about perfection, but about feeling generous to welcome. Because in the end, this is how I want my home to be, a soft place to land for those who walk through its doors.

Practices I'll Continue

Have a guest space ready at all times.

Pick up as I walk through the house.

Make my bed.

Focus on completing the small task in front of me.

Recruit others to help me with cleaning/home management.

Invite the Holy Spirit to be the host in our home.

Questions for Reflection

1. How does your home make you feel today?
2. What small things can you do to move your house further from chaos and more toward peace?
3. Does the idea of the Holy Spirit acting as the host in your home sound strange to you? Why or why not?

Words for My Actual Life

For I was hungry and you gave me something to eat, I was thirsty and you gave me something to drink, I was a stranger and you invited me in. (Matt. 25:35)

MONTH 7

Love Is in the Details

Creativity

Art washes away from the soul the dust of everyday life.

—Pablo Picasso

The Need

For the last month Gracie has been carrying around a plastic shoe box full of crayons. In the car, around the house, into coffee shops. Some broken. A swath of hues. Just in case she has the urge to color, she's prepared. Lalo makes up songs about whatever might be in front of her to act as her muse. We hear them from another room as she plays, singing for no audience in particular, simply for the joy of making a melody. And she dances at church. Not noticing she's the only one.

In a life where the to-do list is urgent and longer than I can overcome, creative pursuits seem optional, even frivolous. And I call myself a writer. But even writing, with its deadlines and editing and contracts, can become a product to be produced rather than a process to relish. Where the end result will be evaluated and reviewed by other people and true vulnerability can be squelched.

So why bother? Why pay attention to something that doesn't meet an immediate need? A few years ago CNN published an article titled "A Creative Life Is a Healthy Life."[1] The article showed there is lowered stress, with all kinds of physical benefits, when we add creativity to our routines. And this makes sense because creativity is woven into the fabric of who we are. God is a "maker," and he made us in his image, to be makers. When I deny that creative part of me, I am going against my very nature. Even if I don't really feel like an "artsy" person, I need to cultivate this part of me to truly thrive on a daily basis. I was made for this, but seldom indulge in intentionally creative pursuits.

The Experiment

I'm bringing the creativity! The poetry. The music. The gardening. The singing (oh help us all). I want to soak in it and remember that the details are what give this life flavor. I want to celebrate those things that others craft and my own unique mark on this world. Like Gracie, I'm going to have my box ready in case I get the urge. And I want to notice the creative work that is already here right in front of me.

My Actual Approach

Participate in a daily creative activity.

Spend time outside every day.

Write for non-work purposes.

DAY 1

I'll admit, I have a bit of an issue around artistic pursuits that I'm sure stems back to my childhood. My father was an artist by profession. A man who, in my developing brain, didn't have time for me. Because he was busy. Making art.

He lived on the other side of the world and would send me art books about himself. When what I wanted was him. His attention. His affection. As an adult I understand life is more complicated than it seems to a ten- or twelve-year-old. And as I've started writing more and I'm aware of my own tendencies to disappear into my work, I'm recognizing that I might be more like my father than I've known before.

Creativity is about doing things with your own flair.

So I suspect early in my development I made an association between *artist* and one who is irresponsible. That creativity is something you should get to once you've finished your obligations. I'm starting the experiment by working on re-understanding what it means to be an artist.

In her book *A Million Little Ways*, Emily Freeman reminds me that the very beginning of the world's story as we know it shows us about who God is and who we are.

> The first thing we know about God is he made art. What is the first thing we know about people? We were made in the image of God.[2]

We were made to create! It is in us, so when we don't allow that part of us to flourish, we wither. Our world becomes a million hues of gray rather than a vibrant, in-living-color place.

If I wait until my must-dos are done, I'll never get to self-expression. Instead I'll live as a robot, replicating the lives of everyone around me. Because creativity is about doing things with your own flair. So I'm getting off to a slow start. I'm focusing on the mental adjustment. No creativity happened unless we count creative thinking.

DAY 2

Sometimes I set others up to be creative. In fact, it's often much easier than doing it for myself. Take today after school on the playground with Heather.

"I'm engaged!"

"What?!" I knew she'd been dating Nels for years now, but I didn't know it was time.

"And we're getting married next month."

"What?!"

Because I'm so eloquent.

Standing next to the climbing wall and slide, I wasn't sure how to react. In fact, I was surprised I was feeling a little sad, so I turned to the practical.

"What can I do? A bachelorette party? Dress shopping? Food? Flowers?"

"I think I'm good. I have a sundress already. We'll have it catered in the backyard."

She could tell I needed a job. And she's a good friend who let it be about me in a moment that was supposed to be all about her.

"Can you hang lights?" she asked.

Right away I knew that was outside my talent pool. I like to work from my strengths, after all. But I happen to know someone who is quite handy and of course I volunteered him.

"Derek can! He can build something! Do you need anything built?"

Again the eloquence is astounding.

"Are you serious?" Well, yeah, I'm serious. I'm all for volunteering other people to do things, especially my husband. "I just need a little platform. Everyone will be standing and I'm so short. Something to raise us up a bit. Do you think he could do that?"

Sounds easy enough. (Easy for me to say, right?)

"Totally. He can totally do that."

DAY 3

I have a handy husband. A creative, artistic handyman. When people first come to our mid-century ranch with its open space and walls torn down and retro details mixed with classic pieces, they compliment me on my style. And I have to admit I have nothing to do with the decorating. Remember, home aesthetics are not my specialty. And along with the embarrassment of not being a good housekeeper is that of having a husband who is the decorator. It seems like a bit of role reversal.

But I've gotten over that in recent years. I embrace that's who he is. That's who I am. I'm not a visual person.

But God has called *me* to be creative too. Not just my husband and my children. And you would think because I'm a writer, considered a creative profession, that I find my creative outlet all the time. I also am coming to terms with that part of who I am. My art for the world comes out in words.

For Derek it's in woodworking.

For my friend Krista it's in food.

For my sister-in-law Kendall it's in painting and fashion and photography and video production and, yes, home decorating.

For my mom it's gardening.

For me it's in words. Vocabulary strung together to elicit pictures and feelings. Sometimes—okay, often—those aren't the creative talents I want. I want what Kendall has. What Derek has. And I can try those outlets for the joy of them, but the truth is, the end result won't be the same.

I'm still working on rethinking creativity.

DAY 5

I've been wondering why I've felt somewhat sad about Heather's news, and I realized today it's because I'd transferred much of my and Derek's relationship onto Heather and Jon's. We were similar in many ways.

Like us, they were young when they married, and they truly liked each other and wanted to be with each other more than anyone else. Even their height difference mirrored ours. When Jon died, all I could think about was what if the same happened to Derek? My grief for Heather was not purely on her behalf; it was tied up in my own what-ifs.

But this is Heather's actual life. After this tragedy, and truly that's not a dramatic overstatement, the circumstances were hers to deal with. And she found love again. She could live in grief and love simultaneously. And that was better than grief alone. I needed to move past my own what-ifs and celebrate with her.

DAY 6

A few weeks ago we purchased tomato plants at the annual school plant sale and managed to plant them in their designated garden plots before they died (unlike last year's poor fellows, which withered in the plastic containers we brought them home in).

Fortunately, the heavy spring rains kept this year's plants alive the last few weeks before we had a chance to plant them.

For my mother, gardening is her creative outlet. She envisions how plants will look in different blooming seasons and digs up and moves what she planted the year before. It's a constant work and an equally constant rework. I would rather not spend my free time that way. I probably fit in the category comedian Jim Gaffigan places himself, that of the "indoorsy."[3] But we have dedicated some of our precious small backyard real estate to a few raised vegetable beds so our city children can see that food actually grows from the ground and doesn't just appear in the grocery store.

So experiment completed with a few tomato plants in the ground and dirt under my fingernails. There is something satisfying for this city girl in all of that. Today, being creative meant getting messy.

DAY 7

Poetry intimidates me.

It's nothing I've studied and therefore I don't feel qualified to write it. And yet as part of this experiment I will be courageous and try. What am I afraid of? When I push through all the feelings, it is simply what others might think. I want to impress people and I'm afraid what I write will be just awful.

But I am trying to be courageous, so I am reading poetry to get inspired and then I will write. Today I read Langston Hughes. Every word so succinctly charged with meaning. Perhaps that's why poetry is intimidating; there are no extra words.

DAY 8

I tried to write a poem today. I visited Six-Word Memoirs,[4] a site I visit often because it shows how a picture or an idea can be expressed in just six words. The topic I chose was "Love," because what else is there? Here are a few attempts with my inner critic attached:

Love: Four babies. Eight arms. Endless hugs. (Cheesy. I can't help it.)

Love: Wrinkles, cellulite, gray hairs, solid marriage. (A bit depressing.)

Love: Eternity encased in one man's skin. (How much said in just six words. In just one man. Still cheesy?)

DAY 9

I'm going to try a real poem today. This is painful, like listening to my own voice on an answering machine (remember those?), but I'm working on not impressing others. I know no rules here, so I'm going with what moves me. Here is my first attempt:

Loving My Actual Life (because what else should be my prompt?)

> 9 months of trial, error, trial again
> This life that often feels like drudgery, must be dusted off
> This everydayness that often runs into the next, must be
> seen afresh
>
> 9 months of knitting, growing, knitting again
> The nausea, tired, oh so tired, and glorious movement
> finally
> The aches, sleep deprivation, heartburn, worth it a million
> times over
>
> 9 months of homework, packed lunches, homework again
> The driving, picking up, meetings and schedules
> The present life that runs the clock that won't stop
>
> 9 months of trial, error, trial again
> This life that I must savor, not slip through my fingers
> today
> Tomorrow's unknown the reminder to appreciate what is

I can't even bear to share this. It feels awkward and exposed, and all my self-doubts are shouting in my head, *This is the worst poem ever! Why are you even trying? Who do you think you are?* Yet I'm giving the gift of going first. If I can disclose my unedited, unschooled, first-draft poem with you, then maybe you can try that one thing that feels intimidating.

As artist Henri Matisse is credited with saying, "Creativity takes courage."

DAY 11

Of all the experiments so far, this is the one I've found myself questioning the most. *Is this really that important?* It doesn't have the screaming urgency of the others and so it quickly gets pushed to the end of the day's to-do list. It is not prioritized in my daily life because, unlike getting people out of the house in the morning or feeding them, I don't see an immediate practical benefit to setting aside time to be creative.

In her book *168 Hours: You Have More Time Than You Think*, Laura Vanderkam notes we are starting to see the drawbacks of overscheduled kids. Amen to that. Two of my four children are allowed to do extracurricular sports and they get only one sport a season and we are still run ragged by the intensity of our family's schedule. But Vanderkam points out our children are not the only ones who need free time to optimize creativity and productivity.

> Adults, likewise, need unstructured time to truly relax and reju-
> venate. Sometimes our best ideas about advancing our careers or
> solving personal problems spring out of these fallow hours. The
> point that I think gets missed in all these lamentations is that almost
> all of us do have adequate time in our 168 hours for play—and for
> the structured leisure activities such as sports, arts, or volunteer
> work that add meaning to life. . . . Because we don't think through
> our leisure time, we often don't even recognize when it's appearing,
> and so we wind up spending big chunks of it in the most friction-
> less way possible: in front of the television.[5]

She says computers can be interchanged with television these days as the go-to mindless fallback that requires nothing from us. Certainly my computer or my phone is much more tempting for me than the television. But it's about making the most of our downtime when we have it. Either to be intentional about a creative pursuit or letting our minds wander instead of inputting the mindless junk food we tend to feast on.

I'm feeling inspired to be a little more intentional here.

DAY 13

Summer break has begun, and a few weeks ago the girls and I made a comprehensive list of all the things we wanted to do. In general I avoid the term "bucket list" because I don't want the pressure of having to get it all done. And it implies we will be checking every single one of these things off the list. My intent was to start thinking about fun, not create stress with more to do. Besides, the whole "things I want to do before I die" associated with a bucket list is a little morbid. So I like to think of it more as a "brainstorming session" (which has a lot of meaning to a three-year-old, if you were curious).

Tie-dye was on the list. Tie-dye, which conjures up images of summer camp and street festivals and aging hippies. It also conjures up images of buckets of hot liquid and a big mess as children carry dye-dripping items through the house. But tie-dyeing is what my girls wanted to do. So we went to the store and bought the supplies a few days ago. I was pleasantly surprised that you can now tie-dye without those hot buckets of dye. But then I couldn't help make it happen because we were having people over and the immediate needs of getting the house ready won out. And each day that went by I was asked if we could do the tie-dye and it was as if I was continuously being reminded that I don't let them do anything fun.

Finally today we laid out the supplies, looked at the directions, picked the designs, and Gabi took over. It is wonderful having a crafty tween in the house. She sat on the back lawn on an old sheet and dyed everyone's shirts. That may be a bit of a cop-out in the experiment, outsourcing creativity, but I'd like to think of it as developing creativity in my girl.

Besides, she *was* good at it. We oohed and aahed and gave all kinds of kudos for the good work. And we now have matching tie-dyed shirts as a family, ready to hit the farmer's market or a drum circle in coordinated style.

DAY 14

Heather's wedding is still two weeks away, but I know how these things go. Weeks quickly disappear without a flicker of warning. And that stage wasn't going to make itself. We went over to Heather's house tonight and Derek talked to her about design. About how many kids there would be on the platform with them, where her dad would stand to officiate. We measured. This was Derek's ultimate sweet spot of creativity, the challenge of a project within parameters. Form meets function. And I was happy to hold the measuring tape.

DAY 15

I went for a walk and made myself notice. Notice what is all around but I'm usually too distracted to see. The pink flowers covering my neighbor's shrubs looked like something my girls would use to make bouquets for their dolls, miniature versions of bigger blooms. Low-hanging branches over the sidewalk, offering shade to those who sneak by or stay awhile. The yellow black-eyed Susans and purple hollyhocks. And so much green grass. A million, billion little blades, as Gracie might say.

It says right there in the Bible that God knows the number of hairs on our head,[6] and if that is true he knows these flower petals and these blades of grass. He has made them in part for my enjoyment.

God, brilliant Lord,
    yours is a household name.
Nursing infants gurgle choruses about you;
    toddlers shout the songs
That drown out enemy talk,
    and silence atheist babble.
I look up at your macro-skies, dark and enormous,
    your handmade sky-jewelry,
Moon and stars mounted in their settings.
Then I look at my micro-self and wonder,
Why do you bother with us?
Why take a second look our way?
Yet we've so narrowly missed being gods,
    bright with Eden's dawn light.
You put us in charge of your handcrafted world,
    repeated to us your Genesis-charge,
Made us lords of sheep and cattle,
    even animals out in the wild,
Birds flying and fish swimming,
    whales singing in the ocean deeps.
God, brilliant Lord,
    your name echoes around the world.[7]

As a mom, I see God's evidence in my children. When they were nursing infants I felt the miracles in my arms. These people who came from nothing and have their own bodies and temperaments and personalities and souls. These living beauties I can't seem to get enough of. They are the evidence of God's creation for me.

But I forget to notice the rest of his creation that surrounds me every day. Those Rocky Mountains that jut up into our Colorado blue sky, the fruits and vegetables and herbs I use to feed my family. I get in my car and drive to my appointed destination. I'm focused on the task and miss the setting, which is half the journey. The relishing, savoring, appreciating God's gifts right here in his natural world are often passed over because of the urgency of the immediate. The phone call I'm on, the arguing in the backseat, my thoughts about the next few hours, or worries about the next few years.

It is indeed easy for me to praise God when I stop and notice the details of what he has created. It is the discipline of stopping that is key.

DAY 17

It's difficult to be inspired when you're exhausted, when literally running from one thing to the next. (I ran into the house today from the driveway. Since when did my life get so busy that running is my required speed?) And so vacation calls. I'm not much of a vacationer, in that I don't take long chunks of time off work. And I'm not married to one either. Partly because our work is mobile, we can access it (or better, it can access us) anytime, anywhere. And partly because our work is indistinguishably woven into who we are and why we feel called to be on this planet at this time. In some ways, we can't separate our work from our essence because it flows out of our beliefs.

But even God—yes, after he made the planets, the animals, and threw some stars into the cosmos—took a vacation and rested. Who do I think I am that the world can't live without me for a few days? Let's be serious. My children, sure, have a difficult time making their own dinners sometimes, but work? It can be put on hold.

> *It is indeed easy for me to praise God when I stop and notice the details of what he has created. It is the discipline of stopping that is key.*

DAY 20

Now, this is vacation.

We're a few days in and there's lots of sleeping in (well, at least as long as our little people allow), eating, sitting on the dock, jumping into the lake, and repeating. Again and again. A nine-day vacation is not in our annual routine, but a family wedding in the Colorado mountains combined with Oma's seventieth birthday week at a lake house she rented for her entire clan is making for a long and leisurely week. And best yet, the internet is slow. So for the most part I'm not trying to respond to emails. I'm working at being present with the sparkle of the sun on the water and the sounds of kids jumping from the dock to the raft.

It's difficult to be inspired when you're exhausted.

This pace allows for the intensity to stop. For the mind to wander.

Last week *Harvard Business Review* reported on a study on vacations and productivity. "Four out of 10 employees say that they can't take their vacation because they have too much work to do. But, think about it this way: Whether or not you take a vacation, you're still going to have a lot of work to do. Life is finite, and work is infinite."[8]

Well, look at that. The *Harvard Business Review* is suggesting we love our actual lives. In fact, the study concludes that those who take vacation are actually more likely to get promoted. Why? Because they are refreshed, and therefore more creative.

No matter if work is in a cubicle or at the kitchen sink, we are made to slow down because that pace change creates thinking change. That essentially is creativity, right?

DAY 21

Board games! I like boundaries and rules and challenges that fit within them. Remember, creativity flourishes within boundaries. But here's the problem. Well, actually, two problems. Derek doesn't like board games and my children spread any kind of multiple-piece anything all over creation so that once a game box is opened at our house, it is almost immediately impossible to play again because half the pieces have gone to live under the couch.

But here on this vacation, my sister-in-law Lindsay brought Beyond Balderdash, a game of creativity where one convinces others of the correct definition of a word or reason for a notable obscure date. (It's more complicated than that, but you get the idea.) Are you kidding me? A game that involves wordsmithing? I would pay to play it.

Tonight as all of the younger cousins watched a movie and the men sat around the campfire, Kendall, Lindsay, and I played with some of the older kids. And the word *sniddle* became the word of the moment. Without looking at each other's answers, we each wrote down our own created definition, and from our collective choices each of us guessed at the real answer. Here are the definitions we came up with and the actual one mixed in:

No matter if work is in a cubicle or at the kitchen sink, we are made to slow down because that pace change creates thinking change.

Sniddle:

> The leather strap on a canteen.
>
> A word in which means u have a body function problem.
>
> A snake attracted to sugar.
>
> Giggling or laughing while eating chocolate peppermint bark.
>
> Very coarse grass.
>
> When you carve flowers into a thick object.

Only one person selected the correct answer (very coarse grass). But the correct answer didn't matter; we were letting our creativity flow. This was simply for fun, to hear a word or a date or an acronym, have no idea what it truly meant, and let our minds wander. Sometimes a part of the word inspired us to go in a certain direction, and sometimes an answer from a previous round sparked something in us that propelled us forward.

Some definitions were plausible and others were crafted simply to make cousins laugh. Both motives were good. Creativity can happen with others. It can be fun. It can be relaxed. It can be half an hour at a time. And it can't be perfect. Perfection tears away at creativity's very nature. It binds it up instead of letting it soar.

DAY 22

In total lake leisure mode, I mentioned this month's experiment to my sister-in-law Kendall. She is the person I know who most embodies creativity. She said, "Creativity is simply an extension of who you are." She said it so naturally, so matter-of-factly, as though she was saying, "It's Thursday" or "Sandwiches are tasty." Because for her, creative pursuits—from how she decorates her home to her work—are natural extensions of who she is.

Perhaps I need to see these extensions of myself—my conversations, relationships, schedule management—as extensions of who I am. Perhaps I need to redefine for myself what creativity actually is. And I will see that I am really already incorporating it more than I realize.

DAY 25

The countdown is on. The wedding is tomorrow and the stage is halfway constructed. I am cutting burlap for the skirt because I can do that. I can't help with the stage, I can't sew, but I can cut like nobody's business.

Do what only you can do.

DAY 26

We really should have had some reality TV show cameras onsite today. Four hours before the wedding guests would be arriving, we were in our garage taking pictures of the set up below the platform and numbering two-by-fours so we could recreate the stage after dismantling it and transporting it a mile and a half from our garage to Heather's backyard. Oh, and it was thirty feet long and involved twenty twenty-pound cinder blocks.

But we did it with the help of friends and Nels and Heather's dad when we arrived. We recreated the stage, staple-gunned the burlap skirt around the edge, finishing about an hour before guests started coming. Barely enough time to run home, shower, change, and get to the wedding on time.

This was a union of two people whose stories included loss, but who were making the most of their actual circumstances. It's not what they would have written twenty years ago, because grief was required to bring them together. But here they were and we celebrated. And Derek tried not to look but couldn't help himself as a flower girl discovered the creaky spot on the stage and rocked back and forth on it. He was sure the whole wedding party was going to come crashing down. They didn't.

> *Creativity can happen with others. It can be fun. It can be relaxed. It can be half an hour at a time. And it can't be perfect.*

Sometimes we feel as though life is crashing down. Heather certainly has. And we find gold and joy in the midst of it. While "reality TV" is manipulated and edited, leaving not an ounce of reality left for us to process, this one life does not allow for a retake. There is no editing crew but our own. This is it.

DAY 28

I took my Bible to my front porch this morning. My coffee in hand, I could tell by the early heat it was going to be a sweltering day. But the sun was still low enough in the east that the temperature was bearable. The birds were talking to each other. It is the quiet time for our city neighborhood. Even at night the occasional siren or car horn or even neighbors yelling cuts any quiet. But the early morning is peace.

Except for the birds.

It is their chance to rule the skies and make plans for the day. To say their greetings and claim their nesting places.

I sat and read and heard one bird's call, distinct from the rest. And then I spotted her on top of the telephone pole, using her voice to greet the world.

Her distinct voice. Set apart. Different from the rest. I wouldn't have heard that voice if she hadn't used it. I'm getting it, Lord, I'm getting it. My creativity only serves God if I exercise it.

What I Learned

I went into this month not realizing that I held high expectations for my own "creativity." I quickly realized I was helping those around me be creative, but hesitant about my own efforts to try something un-prescribed because I didn't want to fall short of amazing, meaningful, memorable creations. I rediscovered creativity is about the process, not the results, and it's certainly about letting go of expectations. It's the letting loose, freedom in being who God called me to be. There is a reason for the term "creative process"—because it is just that.

> My creativity only serves God if I exercise it.

And I faced the truth that I'm envious of other people's talents. I had to actively remind myself that though God made us all creative, he didn't gift us with skills or interests or personalities that are alike. I could be both free in creative expression that didn't come naturally and confident in that which did.

Though I didn't find the practical, life management benefits I have in some of the other experiments, I did see that this is where the richness of life is often found, this making time and space for the creative process. And when I do, I actually might make enough room for a fresh idea that *will* end up helping me in the practical. Or at least will keep me from living like a walking robot and living a little more like a reflection of God's creation. It may help me love this actual life.

Practices I'll Continue

Engage in creative activities that are purely for fun, even silly.

Allow myself to write without expectation of sharing.

Pay attention to God's creation when driving or walking outside.

Try new creative expressions.

Encourage others to use their creative talents for God's purposes.

Questions for Reflection

1. Do you agree with this chapter's opening quote by Pablo Picasso, "Art washes away from the soul the dust of everyday life"? Why or why not?

2. What type of creativity feels natural to you? What type feels intimidating?

3. How do you see God's creativity around you? Is there a way you can see with "new eyes"? How does that make you relish what's right in front of you?

Words for My Actual Life

GOD, brilliant Lord, your name echoes around the world. (Ps. 8:9 Message)

Three Times a Day

Meals

A party without cake is just a meeting.

—Julia Child

The Need

"There's nothing to eat!" "I'm hungry!" "What's for dinner?"

It's a constant request. Actually, a constant demand. The minute I've fed one person, another (or the same one, even) is asking for more. My own tummy grumbles and I realize I skipped breakfast and open a cupboard and stare into the caverns wondering what (*what!*) I can make for lunch.

We end up filling our bellies with whatever we can find. And ravenous foragers are neither a satisfied nor a well-nourished bunch. The junk food route has its place, but when the drive-through becomes the default dinner plan, our energy and budget suffer big time (not to mention our waistlines; some of us have better metabolisms than others around here).

Given the predictable nature of needing three meals a day, why am I constantly surprised when someone wants to know what's for dinner? And don't even get me started about lunches and snacks! I go to the grocery store or Costco and spend hundreds of dollars and the next day can't figure out what to make for people to eat. It is a constant low-level stress that I carry with me every day.

No matter the size of the family, one to twenty members, food needs to be purchased, prepared, consumed, and cleaned up, multiple times a day. According to the USDA, women on average spend 47 minutes per day on food preparation. That's almost an hour, average, for all women![1] Those of us who are feeding other people fall on the long end of the average, so we're surely preparing more than an hour a day. No wonder people have entire businesses, websites, blogs, and books about this very topic. How can I possibly tackle it in a single month?

The Experiment

I recognize two truths about my situation. First, I deal with food preparation all day long. It's an unavoidable part of my schedule. Second, the healthier the food I feed myself and my family, the better everyone feels.

My experiment is simply to make meals and their preparation as enjoyable a process as possible. For one month I will try to make mealtime, even dinnertime for a four-nights-a-week sports family, something that gives me pleasure rather than dread. Of course, I want it to be more streamlined, relationship-centered, delicious, and nutritious, while staying within our family's grocery budget. Possible?

Anything has to be better than the current survival mode.

My Actual Approach

Minimize trips to the grocery store by creating a weekly meal plan.

Have healthy snacks ready.

Set up dinnertime as shared community time.

DAY 1

I must begin with recognizing that this month feels especially heavy on the first world pain category. The fact that I have access to healthy, affordable, varied, fresh food, not to mention clean water, is something I too often take for granted. Women all over the world would be glad to have the problems I do in this department. And many neighbors in my own community don't have this luxury of excess. In 2014, 15.3 million children lived in "food insecure households" in the United States,[2] which means they didn't have access to nutritious food on a regular basis.

So Month 8 simply starts with gratitude.

Lord, I do not understand why I am in a place and time where I don't have to worry when or if my children will eat. Help me to be grateful for what you have given me. Thank you for the water and the nutrition available to make my body work so I can more fully live for you and your purposes. Amen.

I already feel better about the goodness right in front of me. I'm appreciating what I have and sitting in that for today.

DAY 2

It's time to get serious about how I'm going to approach food and its preparation in a more sustainable way for the Kuykendalls. It's time to get organized. Out comes the calendar thingy from downstairs. The one with all the rainbow colors and sticky notes that I was sure was going to help me get the house organized. I knew it would come in handy. I just didn't know it would be for meal planning. But it is perfect! Every poster-sized page acts as a week with spots for four meals: breakfast, lunch, dinner, and snacks. (Because sometimes snacks are what completely put me over the edge in the "I'm hungry" category.) I keep telling myself it will be better if I have a plan.

All the home-management gurus say you should do this kind of thing. And I've had phases, especially when I've been extra busy and motivated to be organized, when I've been great at it. When I've planned out four to five dinners and done a single grocery shopping trip for all of them! It's such a novel idea, isn't it?

My friend Krista is my personal meal-planning mentor. She is a gourmet, plans well, and feeds people out of love. But one thing she says that helps with meal planning is to know what you are having for dinner by 10:00 a.m.

In her book *Reclaiming Home*, Krista says, "When we are prepared, we save ourselves from the last minute scramble, save money, and have the satisfaction of providing a healthy meal for our family."[3] Does it mean I have all the ingredients in my kitchen? That's better, but even if I don't, at least I have a plan and can hit the grocery store on the way home from preschool pick-up, which eliminates some of that low-lying stress that follows me around.

Unsure why I felt overwhelmed, I decided to focus on just the weekend. I don't have to plan everything we're going to eat forever, just tonight and tomorrow. Beginning with the few days right in front of me would give me the plan before 10:00 a.m. And I didn't want to go to the grocery store three times in the next three days; I have other things to do!

I don't have to plan everything we're going to eat forever, just tonight and tomorrow.

Gabi plopped next to me on the dining room bench (because that's what tweens do; they don't sit gently; they sit with vigor) as I sat with my computer going back and forth between my screen with the family's rainbow colored calendar and Pinterest. Gabi offered ideas (or rather approval of the plan), Derek was within earshot, and I made myself start. The calendar was key so I knew what each day held. *Where will we be coming from? What kind of prep time will I have before the meal? Will there be any leftovers from the night before?*

But guess what? I planned one night and then the next. And as I got ideas and inspiration, I plugged them into the spaces where the time worked and pinned them to my newly created "My People Are Hungry" board.

Pulled pork sandwiches were Gabi's request for dinner. We didn't have the long lead-time tonight that it required, but on Wednesday, when we'd be gone all afternoon, the Crock-Pot could be doing its work. My planning for the weekend had now extended well into next week.

A list. A shopping trip. A plan.

DAY 3

I made muffins (from a mix) this morning. And eggs. And bacon. It was all written on my big calendar and it was the plan. Because I have a plan and I'm working it.

But I also had my first glitch. I slept in until 9:00 a.m. I haven't slept in until 9:00 with all four kids in the house . . . ever. I mean it. Ever. Even with the flu or with a baby up all night nursing. Never, ever. And so this Sunday morning when I planned a big breakfast believing we'd have all this extra time before church, I was rushed. But because I had a plan and I'd shopped, it happened.

And then home from church to make tuna sandwiches on slider buns with chips.

At both meals my children declared that I was making "fancy food." Yes, tuna with mayonnaise, relish, lime juice, and a little salt and pepper apparently constitutes fancy at our house. You'd think I'd never made tuna sandwiches before. But it was the plan that allowed for the presentation (I'm guessing) that made it feel special. And oh how good it felt to leave church with everyone hungry and be able to say, "I have stuff for lunch ready at home." I was the hero of the moment.

It really is the little things.

> We don't have to be afraid of overloving or oversharing God's goodness because there is always more.

DAY 4

At church yesterday our pastor Jill talked about the theology of abundance rather than the theology of scarcity. The idea that there is always enough room at God's table for more. More people. More servings of grace. That we don't have to be afraid of overloving or oversharing God's goodness because there is always more.

For many of us, Jill included, the idea of scarcity is real (as real as it can be here in the United States). She grew up in a home with a budget. As a parent now, I'm realizing that the life lessons a strict budget offers are a good thing. Knowing that resources are limited helps us take care of what we've been given, use it wisely, and not be wasteful, and helps us be more empathetic to those who have less than we do. But what if our focus on limitations results in a tendency toward scarcity and holding back?

Freedom can come from a simple meal plan.

Sometimes I limit my idea of what God can offer because I want to be grateful for what I have. Is it not clear in "Give us today our daily bread," straight from the Lord's Prayer,[4] that we are to ask for today's portion when praying?

As a result, I limit my understanding of the possibilities. There has to be a balance. Being grateful for the mercy and grace offered right here, right now, and believing God can do even more.

There is always room at the table.

DAY 5

"Mom, what's for breakfast?"

"Smoothies and eggs."

Nothing extravagant or complex, but I have an answer! No more staring in the open fridge and wondering. Not to mention, this dinner plan by 10:00 a.m. thing is liberating. I'm unaware of the stress decisions around food create until I remove them from the mix. And now I walk around like this roast-beef-sized weight has been lifted from my shoulders. The last few days I've known what freedom can come from a simple meal plan.

DAY 6

I can't help but think in terms of the theology of abundance in context of food. Terms like *harvest* and *bounty* connect God's lavish provision with the things we eat. From the very beginning of his holy texts, the very first chapter of the very first book, he reminds us of the goodness and abundance of his harvest.

> Then God said, "I've given you
>   every sort of seed-bearing plant on Earth
> And every kind of fruit-bearing tree,
>   given them to you for food.
> To all animals and all birds,
>   everything that moves and breathes,
> I give whatever grows out of the ground for food."
>   And there it was.
>
> God looked over everything he had made;
>   it was so good, so very good!
> It was evening, it was morning—
>   Day Six.[5]

And not just for us people, but for the animals too.

And that was it. The food making was his last task of Creation. The next verse says,

> Heaven and Earth were finished,
>   down to the last detail.
> By the seventh day
>   God had finished his work.[6]

Then he rested. That sounds familiar, doesn't it? Dinner is often my last duty of the day before I collapse. If my life aims to reflect God in all aspects, perhaps a little rest after cooking is in order.

It doesn't say have a glass of wine and watch Netflix, but that's what rest often looks like at the end of the day at my house.

DAY 8

The pool offers fun, but it rarely offers nutritious eats. The snack bar sells licorice ropes with a shelf life of about twenty-three years and corn dogs the lifeguards microwave to order. Helpful in a pinch, I'll admit, but not real sustenance and usually a post-snack tummy ache is involved. So I need to pack for my crew before we hit the pool. And, well, I'm just always surprised how many snacks are required for all of us to be happy. But here are two things I've found: everyone is less grumpy when their tummies are full and it's pretty hard to whine when there's food in your mouth.

> *I am always—yes, always—glad when I've had the forethought to bring some food (and some water too).*

"Mom, I'm bored."

"Here. Stick an apple in it."

"Mom, I'm hungry."

"I have just the thing for you. Carrots and pretzel thins and hummus."

Rarely in my life have I been a snack-prepared mom, but I am always—yes, always—glad when I've had the forethought to bring some food (and some water too).

DAY 10

I went to Costco and spent $400. And I have nothing to make for dinner. Unless of course we want to have Gatorade, Cheez-Its, and Go-GURTs. Part of the cost is having twenty people over tomorrow for a barbecue. But I am realizing if I don't have a plan at this buy-everything-in-bulk store, I will come home with cartloads of snacks (which are a good thing when we are hungry in between meals, just not at breakfast time) and paper products.

My new plan: Cover the same items we eat over and over for breakfast, lunch, and snacks by buying in bulk at Costco. Buy specific ingredients for dinner plans at the local market.

DAY 11

The Dale House staff came for dinner. The Dale House, the place where Derek and I fell in love and knew we were meant to make meals together for a lifetime. Where kids aging out of the foster care system or finishing a criminal sentence live until they turn eighteen. Where my friend Sharon taught me to cook for twenty at a time, so I always over-make when we have people over. Dale, the middle name of one of our girls, because this place is God's kingdom being worked out here on earth and the starting place of our family's story.

Nearly every year we've lived in Denver this constantly changing group of wholehearted people drive up from Colorado Springs for an afternoon Rockies baseball game and then to our house for a cookout. And it's true the menu is just a walk through Costco these days. Burgers, brats, buns, chips, pickles, watermelon, corn on the cob, and green salad. And this year ice cream cones for dessert. Nothing fancy, but we want to offer them our best. And we offer it with abundance.

May our table (or lawn or chairs around our backyard) be a place where these friends we don't know by name, but we know by shared mission, can be nourished and celebrated. Here are people who live with teenagers who have committed crimes and are aging out of foster care, to give them one last shot at family before they're on their own. If anyone deserves a good burger it's this crew.

Cleaned house. Shopped. Prepped. It took two days and they stayed no more than a couple of hours before they needed to move on to the night shift back in the Springs, sleeping on the floor and sofas outside of kids' rooms.

And Sharon brought us a Chick-fil-A gift card as a thank-you for hosting, so that's like giving us a whole meal's plan right there.

DAY 12

Leftovers really are our friend post party. Brats, buns, salad for dinner.

And then houseguests arriving after dinner. Houseguests who have special requests when it comes to food. The Diet Coke is waiting for them in the fridge and we will shop together the next day to get what everyone wants. Sometimes including others in the meal planning is best. It's not always convenient, and certainly not efficient, but as Sharon reminded me just yesterday, as we were dishing up dinner, the most important things never are.

DAY 13

The rainbow-colored calendar-sticky-note thing is blank this weekend. It's up to guests to help us with the menu. And it includes trips to the store together, which offers an outing. And we went out to dinner tonight, the grown-ups. A splurge that my mom treated us all to. Where kids had hot dogs at home (more leftovers from the barbecue) and we relished being together over North Denver Mexican food and margaritas. This is a plan I can stick with.

DAY 14

I've had years, as in months and months and months, when I've gone to the grocery store with a calculator. When food budgeting was strict and having a special meal was something to be saved for and cherished. I've done major couponing—I mean hours upon hours of cutting—where I followed a system and spreadsheets printed out in the order of the grocery store aisles were involved. Let's just say I know what tight is. And I also know we've never gone hungry. Ever.

A few years ago a mom visiting our MOPS group talked about living with friends for a season. Her husband had been unemployed for months and another family invited them in to live together. One day my new friend used up the last bit of peanut butter in the jar and her hostess sent her to the garage, the extra pantry, to get a replacement. Sitting around our MOPS table, this mom described how she opened the cupboard door and wept. Because it felt like such an over-the-top abundance to simply walk into the garage and find more.

This theology of abundance is about loaves and fishes, about Jesus multiplying what little we have and feeding the masses.[7] This famous story is again the use of food to show he offers more than we need; he offers enough. I'm getting it. I think I'm getting it. With little there is more than enough.

> With little there is more than enough.

Though I haven't always been in the phase of plenty, I am now. I have a little extra in the budget so I can stock up when needed. I have the cushion to buy two of something when it's on sale, knowing it will save me money in the end to buy double in the moment. But the funds need to be there to be able to do that.

I never, ever, want to take God's provision for granted.

Lord, help me today to see and understand how much you offer in the food at our table. Help me to give you thanks when I open the cupboard door and reach for the cereal box, knowing if we run out I will have other food to give my children. Thank you. Thank you. Thank you. And Lord, I pray for mothers everywhere who worry where their children's next meal might come from. I do not understand why I have so much. I often focus on what is lacking. Help me to see what I do indeed have. Amen.

DAY 17

The freezer is our friend. The freezer is our friend. Here's the thing about sticking with the 10:00 a.m. plan: you have enough time to take something out of the freezer and have it defrost by dinnertime. Tonight's yumminess that required ten minutes of prep time other than the grill? Brats and Italian sausage (defrosted from the freezer), freshly baked pull-apart rolls (I had dough in the freezer), and tomatoes (from our garden) with olive oil, salt, and fresh dill (all found in the kitchen). Not a lot of prep time needed, but we had to plan two of the three items ahead of time for proper defrosting. It allowed us to have meat and fresh bread days after going to the store.

DAY 18

It is becoming evident to me that I'm much more interested in the people at my table than I am in the food being served. That's okay. In a month-long experiment all about food preparation or at least food planning, it's good to recognize that about myself. That doesn't mean those who love the process of feeding others aren't doing it out of care for them. Krista, meal planner extraordinaire, does it so well because it is her love language. A way to love people.

I'm just realizing I enjoy the conversation when people sit down together but it's a little difficult for them to sit if they have empty plates. Meals are a means to an end for me.

Jesus and the table go together. He sat at people's homes and ate with them because it was a way for him to honor them. So it wasn't so scandalous that people invited him in; it was more that he accepted their invitations. Tax collectors who were seen as the corrupt thieves of their day, women who automatically were second class to their male counterparts, those people who had a veil of shame over them because of the status they were born into or the choices they'd made. And by Jesus saying yes to eating with them he was saying yes to honoring them.

Jesus and the table go together.

> *Lord, let me be the one who honors. Who not only invites, but says yes to the invitations that make me uncomfortable. That by allowing others to serve me, I am giving them a chance to show hospitality. Amen.*

DAY 19

All over the world eating and celebrating are intertwined. No matter the culture, traditions of hospitality almost certainly involve food.

Rob came for dinner tonight. He was in town for a conference, and we hadn't seen him since his family returned from their year-long Argentinean adventure where he'd quit his job, they rented a house, and Erica taught English. They were living the life I imagined as a girl, because that was the life I lived as a girl.

> *No matter the culture, traditions of hospitality almost certainly involve food.*

And as he talked about the intensity of friendships they made while they were there, he described the settings for much of the relationship building. They involved meals and parties that went well into the early morning. To the point that Erica, his wife, is researching how to build an Argentinean grill, a *parilla*, in their Portland backyard. In part so they can recreate the atmosphere, not just the food, that they miss. Because here in the US we are a run-around culture, and sometimes we need to sit and eat until the wee hours of the morning to coagulate (if we can stay awake for it, that is).

DAY 20

A typical breakfast when we are in a hurry includes cereal with milk or frozen waffles toasted and served with syrup or jam. *Oh, carbs and sugar to get your day going?* you say. *To have your energy flop about an hour after you eat?* I know it's not a well-thought-out approach. It's a "throw people food, any food, to fill tummies" approach.

So in an attempt to give people energy that will last a little longer, eggs for breakfast is my new thing. They take five minutes to make and offer protein, energy to my kids for the first part of the day. They don't stink up the house like bacon does (but God bless bacon always, right?), and they aren't too expensive.

Though breakfast is the "most important meal of the day," Jesus was pretty clear our energy is not to come from breakfast alone.

"Jesus answered . . . , 'It takes more than bread to stay alive. It takes a steady stream of words from God's mouth.'"[8] Our energy, our protein to sustain our hearts throughout the day, comes from him. And not just him, but his words. More and more I'm realizing God is available to me for energy and sustenance through the Bible.

The Bible has sometimes intimidated me. Jesus frequently speaks in cryptic words, not answering the questions being asked. The language feels awkward. And there are so many lists of names. In fact—I am completely serious here—there was a time when I almost always fell asleep reading it, so I began to pull it out when insomnia hit as my own sleeping pill.

Yet the more I open this book and read it, the more nourished I feel. Because it is God's way of speaking to me! *Why? Why don't I get this?*

DAY 21

I'm back at standing in the kitchen, the cupboard doors swung open, staring at three bags of half-consumed chips, some cans of tomato paste, and a jar of pickles from 2002. Let's just say things have not been going well. The cupboards are bare.

When we arrived home from church I saw a window of opportunity. Four hours ahead of me with nothing planned. Now there was plenty to do (there always is), but nothing on our calendar; nothing with a deadline.

Some quick recipe searches on Pinterest, a trip to the grocery store, and a few hours later I'd prepped four dinners. Three were meats marinating in the freezer and dinner was prepped for tonight when I'd get home from a quick airport run to pick up Nonna and Grandpa. A watermelon and pineapple chopped for snacks.

Get out of town! The sense of satisfaction was almost more than I could bear. I know what's for dinner and I've already done the work!

I walked in the door from the airport and sautéed the steak and broccoli stir-fry. A few minutes later and my people were gobbling it down. That planning and executing would have been success enough. But what surprised me was how much my family kept thanking me. We've been living off of leftovers and pieced-together meals. They associated me being in the kitchen all afternoon with the food in front of them. Do I think they want me acting as their constant personal chef? No. But I do think knowing I put some effort into the planning and preparation made them feel loved (and probably made the actual food a little better).

DAY 22

Cooking itself should be a pleasure, no? If I have to do it every single day I should be creating a space that is both welcoming and easy to use. So today I cleaned and organized my kitchen cabinets and drawers. Because a clean workspace is not only a practical help, offering more room to spread out, but it creates space to be inspired.

And then the event of preparing food itself can be made more fun. Some music, candles, a glass of wine. Why not celebrate God's bounty right here? Today?

DAY 23

We ate in the backyard tonight. The girls asked, but even the little bit of effort to move all the plates fifty more feet past the dining room table to the patio sounded like more work than I wanted to put in. But they promised to help in all of the carrying in and out of the house. And as we sat under the glow of the strings of lights, I thought what a difference a small change made.

Dining al fresco transformed our dinner from a chore to an event.

DAY 25

We're going camping!

Spencer is hitting Southern Colorado in the next few days and it's our one chance to cheer him on in person. Jen, who works at Prov, is joining him to ride for a week and we're taking the new-to-us circa 1985 pop-up trailer to meet them in Walsenburg, Colorado, to take them out to dinner and then camp for a few days. (Never heard of Walsenburg? That's okay, I hadn't either.)

And there is nothing like meal planning and camping. It's meal planning 2.0 because there is no backup plan. No grocery store to run and get that extra ingredient, plus lack of refrigeration needs to be taken into account. I'm ready for the challenge. Why? Because I want to look Spencer in the eye and tell him we're proud of him. And camping time is precious, uninterrupted, confined to a small space, and undistracted-by-encumbrances time as a family.

Dining al fresco transformed our dinner from a chore to an event.

It helps that I have my camping menu staples. We tend to eat the same food on every trip, so it takes the guesswork out of what to make.

DAY 27

"I can't go."

Derek's words when he came home last night. He didn't look at me. I'm sure he was afraid of disappointing the girls, who have spent the last two days playing in the pop-up parked in our driveway while it aired out.

"This is where I'll sleep. And this is where Gracie will sleep. Mommy, where are you sleeping?" Giulianna's favorite activity as she toured and retoured the twenty square feet.

Too much is up in the air on the new Prov house, the very thing Spencer is riding for, so Derek can't leave.

"We'll still go," I blurted.

"What?"

"The girls and I. We won't camp." A little bit of stating the obvious right there. Who was I kidding? He knew that already. "But I'll drive down and meet them for dinner."

I could tell Derek was unsure.

"This is our one chance to see him while he's riding. I want him to know we're rooting for him."

"Are you sure?"

"Yes, it will be an adventure." I'm into those now. Besides, I wanted to free up Derek to do his part in making the house happen. My part was the cheerleader on the sidelines.

The bonus to canceling the camping plans is we already had food ready to go for dinner. Burritos and s'mores at the fire pit in the backyard.

> *Today I choose fun. . . . If I can say yes, I will.*

DAY 28

And this morning breakfast is served in the pop-up trailer parked in the driveway.

It's my one chance to make this morning special. To take those thwarted camping memories and turn them into driveway memories. Because these are the circumstances we have to work with. I can choose to be bummed our plans have changed or I can make the most of them. Today I choose fun.

They want breakfast in the pop-up? If I can say yes, I will.

DAY 29

We drove three hours south to Walsenburg, population 2,896,[9] to meet up with Jen and Spencer. More camping food in the car. Gabi made peanut butter and jelly sandwiches and passed them back to her sisters while I drove to what felt like a ghost town.

We arrived to check out our restaurant options before checking into the only motel and found there was one restaurant open. That made the decision easy. The cyclists pulled in earlier than we expected at 4:00 and were understandably famished after seventy miles of riding, including through a Colorado afternoon thunderstorm. So we ate dinner at 4:00.

"Have whatever you'd like," I said to Jen and Spencer.

As I've said, we don't eat out often. But there are times to celebrate. To splurge. To feast. And there was no better reason for our family to do so than right there. A celebration of the day's ride. Of sobriety. Of community lived out together. Of grace offered and lives rescued. We were celebrating so much more than a cross-country bike trip. We were thanking God for new beginnings through him.

> There are times to celebrate. To splurge. To feast.

Ours was a feast of steak and mashed potatoes. Of appetizers and dessert. Of lavish love that is undeserved and where there is always more room at the table.

DAY 30

We arrived home from our single-night road trip adventure, bellies full of fast food on the drive back. We'd pulled off the freeway twice because of tornado and flash flood warnings. The last hour of my drive I clenched the steering wheel and prayed us through the wet.

As I tucked girls into bed, Derek came into the littles' room and handed me his phone. On the screen was a text, one he'd been waiting for. A large, very large, gift had come through for the new house. The tears came straight from my heart out of my eyes. I was overflowing with gratitude. Loaves and fishes. There is plenty for God's work to be completed in this world.

What I Learned

I went into this month's experiment expecting primarily practical tips. Menus, time savers, miracle tricks to duplicating food

> There is plenty for God's work to be completed in this world.

or getting little people to not whine about how hungry they are when in the car. And yet what I found rather than the tips, though there were some, was the extravagant provision God offers. In our food, both its quality and its quantity, and in his goodness.

Over and over the idea of the table and food is used in the Bible to explain how God cares for us and we are to care for others. And there's not a running out; it's a spilling over, so much we can't run out. When I set my table or open my cupboard with this balance of expectation and gratitude, my meals and their preparation are different.

Nourishment of body and soul are difficult to separate, which is probably why Scriptures connect the two so frequently. When we care for people's bodies with the simple gesture of feeding them we are recognizing their finite, human side. When we offer them our attention we are recognizing their eternal side.

Practices I'll Continue

Know what's for dinner by 10:00 a.m.

Meal plan (and shop) for four days at a time.

Make enough for a few more friends to join or to freeze for another day.

Eat outside.

Celebrate special (and ordinary) occasions with special meals.

Questions for Reflection

1. Which meal of the day is the most difficult for you to manage? What is one thing you can do to improve how you plan and execute that meal?

2. How do you see relationships and meals being connected?
3. When have you experienced God's abundance of loaves and fishes?

Words for My Actual Life

Give us today our daily bread. (Matt. 6:11)

MONTH 9

I Am Made to Do Great Things

Passions

Use me, God. Show me how to take who I am, who I want to be, and what I can do, and use it for a purpose greater than myself.

—Dr. Martin Luther King Jr.

The Need

There is no question I could fill up my days with the "shoulds" on my to-do list. I have dishes and laundry and meals and carpool every day. I try to fit in exercise and work and all the other elements of taking care of people that can consume my waking hours. Oh yes, and then sleep. Every piece of me can be taken by what needs to be done and I can go entire days without doing what I feel I was made to do.

Even mothering, the parts of the job I want to cherish, spending time with my girls and soaking up where they are today, can get overrun with the immediate demands. I know this idea of paying attention to what I love to do can feel like a luxury, but if I don't pay attention to it I can quickly move from gratitude for this life to resentment of others' needs.

There is something wired in each of us that wants to live on purpose for a purpose. Some of our great cultural icons have spoken on passion. From Nelson Mandela, who said, "There is no passion to be found playing small—in settling for a life that is less than the one you are capable of living," to Steve Jobs: "You have to be burning with an idea, or a problem, or a wrong that you want to right. If you're not passionate enough from the start, you'll never stick it out."[1] It's about something bigger than here and now. It's about possibilities. And it's about what we are each driven to work toward.

This is an area of my life I've considered in depth. *What am I committed to? More importantly, what is God calling me to?* And in the last year especially, I've had a renewed interest in these questions. The answers have been fluid and I need to keep asking and re-asking. Because what is true one month isn't necessarily true the next. But even when I've felt certain, where there's been an inner drive and I know what I am working for, I still need to make the time within the limits of a 24-hour day and 7-day week. There is no desert island to which I can escape. I must make this happen within the limitations of my actual life.

The Experiment

I step back from the "crazy busy" life lest it make me crazy. I pay attention to what gives me a larger purpose in this world. That thing that makes me say, "I'm made for this!" It's almost as if the last eight months' worth of experiments have been making room for this one. Because this is a culmination of the things I hold most dear.

A few years ago I interviewed author Shauna Niequist.[2] She said rather than trying to figure out what she is called to do for her entire life, she tries to break the question down into smaller time chunks. *What am I uniquely called to do this year? Or even this month?* It's less overwhelming and takes the pressure off if we consider these questions in more manageable next steps.

The more specific I can be about the "what" can be helpful too. Defining a few areas of purpose and then asking, what can I do about these three things, say, in the next month? Which is exactly how I'm framing this month's experiment. I'm choosing three areas to focus on. How in the next month can I focus on writing as a messenger of hope, supporting Derek in his work at Prov, and being present for my girls as they move from this stage to the next?

That might seem like I've already done the hard work, the figuring out my passions in the first place, and in some ways I have. But I find implementing these areas of passion into my daily life a different, yet still real, kind of challenge. It requires an intentionality that is about prioritizing. Because the challenge for me isn't actually doing these things; I love doing them. It's making the time and space in my life for them.

My Actual Approach

Write in three-hour chunks three days a week.

Complete tasks at home that will free Derek's attention so he can focus on work.

Get school supplies and schedules in order for the new school year.

DAY 1

Lalo turns four this week. There is nothing like my baby, my last born, not being a baby anymore to remind me that time keeps moving. I'm writing today in the clock tower at the university a mile from my house, where I often sit for a few hours of quiet to work. And as I sat down at the desk with a view of the school's quadrant displayed through the face of the clock, the maintenance crew arrived and turned back the clock's hands. Something was not right with how time was moving, and just like that they manipulated it. Hours already spent, now back. Like it was as simple and easy as pushing the hands forward and backward.

I don't have that luxury. I see this girl, this youngest in our family, growing before my eyes. The first birthday with no more diapers, with everyone able to write their own name and speak in full sentences. It is a wake-up call that this life does not stop. And if I do not stop to notice what is right here, tomorrow it may be gone.

A perfect reminder as I begin this month of pursuing what is most important to me. For me it's my little brood. My people right under the same roof. And yet am I really making my daily, hourly decisions with that priority matrix in mind?

DAY 2

Do you want to go see Spencer cross the Brooklyn Bridge?

A text to Derek and me from our friend Denise offering us tickets to fly to New York to welcome Spencer to his final destination. Derek was apprehensive. In the review process for the new young adult home with the city, it seemed to him like an awful time to leave town. I looked at the family calendar and paused. We would be gone the weekend before school started for the three olders. How was my resolve to be living from my priorities from just a day earlier fitting in here? Gracie was starting kindergarten and I needed us all to do that well. Could I get home Sunday evening and create a sense of calm and peace for her?

And here lies the rub when multiple passions seem to collide. When we are forced to make decisions between more than one very good thing. I've spent a year saying no to opportunities outside of my family because I've felt God's call for this time to be focused on the home front. But part of this year's call has also been supporting Derek and his team around this new home. Supporting Spencer's ride has been a tangible way to do this. So perhaps this trip is too?

DAY 3

It's all about birthdays at our house, and Lalo turning four means presents and doughnuts in the morning. And cake at the pool with grandparents, cousins, and a few friends in the afternoon. Because we interrupt this week, this month, this year to celebrate one person. Just for being alive. I love birthdays because I love people. And birthdays are a celebration of life.

I said it already, but I don't mind reiterating the underlying message of celebrating *who* someone is rather than *what* they've done is something I'm all for. Almost every other thing kids (and adults) are celebrated for is centered on accomplishments. Birthdays are a celebration of God's creation. God made you and we are grateful for it and celebrate it. No perfect attendance, or best hitting record, or most revenue brought in. This is about you being uniquely you.

So I push aside the temptations to go overboard on birthday parties to impress people and try to figure out how the birthday person of honor would like to be celebrated. And I find my kids tend to be pretty straightforward. Lalo wanted a pool, a few significant friends, and cake. She chose a Little Mermaid theme (for which I did go down a bit of a Pinterest rabbit trail, I admit, but just on some snack items, nothing crazy). And we went to the pizza place down the street for dinner because it felt special and she likes to pretend like she's playing the video games there.

> Birthdays are a celebration of God's creation. God made you and we are grateful for it and celebrate it.

The only four-year-old birthday she'll ever have. Not to put the mom pressure on, but to take enough time to make it feel noticed, make her feel noticed, in our very busy lives.

DAY 5

A total failure-as-a-mother day. Okay, maybe not a total failure, but a partial one for sure. In fact, let me reframe that altogether. I'm not a failure as a mom. I'm allowed to have bad moments. Which is great because I have a lot of them.

We can't seem to get chores done around our house without bickering, and sometimes that bickering escalates to yelling and sometimes that yelling comes from adults—I mean an adult, singular.

I needed to hold kids to the expectations and in the process did a terrible job of modeling mature handling of emotions. Did the laundry get folded and put away? Yes. Did I snap right back to my child when she complained? Certainly. It's in these littlest of moments where I have opportunity to respond well or not so well. As my friend Meghan says, "Life is big in the little."

And as the apostle Paul says as plain as day,

If I speak with human eloquence and angelic ecstasy but don't love, I'm nothing but the creaking of a rusty gate.

If I speak God's Word with power, revealing all his mysteries and making everything plain as day, and if I have faith that says to a mountain, "Jump," and it jumps, but I don't love, I'm nothing.

If I give everything I own to the poor and even go to the stake to be burned as a martyr, but I don't love, I've gotten nowhere. So, no matter what I say, what I believe, and what I do, I'm bankrupt without love.[3]

It's small moment after small moment that makes up the hours of our days. Yes, these are the ones I need to pay attention to. (And give myself a little grace when they don't go exactly as I planned.)

DAY 6

I'm reverting back to my friend Karen's advice of "Do what only you can do." It really is the best there is.

DAY 7

I may have it too easy on this month's experiment. Writing is what rejuvenates me. Makes me feel like I'm speaking into the world and shaping it in the most effective way. It helps that I'm finishing up this book. I have a deadline. With a contract. It kind of forces me to stick to my experiment.

I've discovered having someone else depend on my follow-through is a big help. I commit to writing something with a date attached to my commitment. I promise one of my children I will play with her in an hour and for an hour. (I not only need to commit to when it will happen, but sometimes for how long as well.) If I don't build in this accountability, often the hours, and then the days, get sucked away with the shoulds and not with the priorities.

> *It's small moment after small moment that makes up the hours of our days.*

189

Today I put dinner with friends on our calendar for weeks out. I will commit so that I'll follow through.

DAY 9

I need to make a decision about the New York trip. It's this nagging question of how I choose between two good things. My fallback is prayer. Because God holds the long view. He certainly knows where I've been, but he also has a vision for where I'm headed and he sees my life holistically, not compartmentalized as I often do. Sometimes those prayers result in my holding back on commitments, like this last year, but sometimes they are a marching order to go forward.

This is just a little weekend away from the kids (in New York City, though; I can't act like it's no big deal), but in light of this experiment I know it represents a bigger question: where is God calling me? I fully believe he can call me to more than one place at a time. He holds it all. He understands what my kids need. What my husband needs. So I go to him with that question: *Lord, what now? Where do you want me to be now?* And I ask that question in the conceptual often, but where is he calling me in the specific, for this particular weekend with these particular circumstances? You know, my actual weekend in my actual life?

So I ask God for direction and the billboard still isn't revealed as I drive down the highway. You know, the one with big instructions, clear and easy to read that say, "Alex, do this." It is the real-life tension of discerning where I am meant to spend my hours.

DAY 10

"Is there something I can do today to help you?" It's one strategy I haven't used enough in my married life, but when I have he has always been grateful.

It's not genius or innovative. It's a simple question, but one that indicates I'm living from my priorities one day at a time. Derek can look around the house and see all that needs to be done. He has access to our family calendar and knows all the places I have to be. I think that makes him feel even more loved, that amid my crazy, I'm stopping, looking at him, and asking, "What about you?"

So I used it today. I actually used it as a "we" since Gracie was sitting next to me and she also had a long summer day ahead of her. Besides, including her in my language implied to her this posture of service was expected of her too.

"Well, I just like being asked." His cheeky tone indicated he was joking, but then he got a bit more serious. "You could pay these bills."

He looked down at the pile of papers on the kitchen counter in front of him. The papers that had been there for almost a week because I said he needed to deal with them. I could do that. Do that for him. In fact, I was the only one who could support him in that way today. Sometimes passion isn't sexy. It's faithful. Sometimes it is paying the bills so the other person can check it off their mental to-do list and focus on what they are called to that day.

Sometimes passion isn't sexy. It's faithful.

Not always, but sometimes.

DAY 13

I can feel the summer days whittling away. I took the girls to Walmart yesterday with my phone in hand, their school supply lists pulled up. As a girl I loved back-to-school and the pencils and Trapper Keepers and calculators. I always saw the school year as the real beginning of the year, and fall represented all things new. A fresh start.

But as a mom, back-to-school has begun to feel like a loss, another summer gone, never to get back. That the time passed is something to grieve rather than the time forward something to anticipate. I don't want to offer that perspective to my kids, that I am grieved that they are growing up. But I *am* grieved they are growing up. It's as if water is slipping through my fingers.

> *Our most difficult choices are between two good things.*

So I'm putting my computer away today. In my basement office where I won't be tempted to open it and reply to one more email or check one more Facebook post. I am going to believe that carpe diem—ness of my life is right now. This is my passion. This life that I am living here and now. If I measure passion by what I feel strongly about, I will say the right here and now is it. These people under my roof, under my care. I am called to love them well. Today.

DAY 14

As I scrolled through my Twitter feed, a TED talk caught my attention: "How to Make Hard Choices." As I started listening, the presenter, Ruth Chang, asked the audience to think of a hard choice.

> Chances are, the hard choice you thought of was something big, something momentous, something that matters to you. . . . But I think we've misunderstood hard choices and the role they play in our lives. Understanding hard choices uncovers a hidden power each of us possesses. What makes a choice hard is the way the alternatives relate. In any easy choice, one alternative is better than the other. In a hard choice, one alternative is better in some ways, the other alternative is better in other ways, and neither is better than the other overall.[4]

Yes! Our most difficult choices are between two good things. And they are not always the big, life-changing decisions; they are the everyday little ones. But it's that every day, over and over, small decision-making that helps us define our road. Ms. Chang goes on to say,

> Far from being sources of agony and dread, hard choices are precious opportunities for us to celebrate what is special about the

human condition, that the reasons that govern our choices as correct or incorrect sometimes run out, and it is here, in the space of hard choices, that we have the power to create reasons for ourselves to become the distinctive people that we are.[5]

God has given us this choice-making ability to say yes to this and no to that. Perhaps when stuck with two good options another question to ask is, God, *which choice will better propel me toward being the person I want to become? That you want me to become?*

DAY 16

I went to speak to a writing group last night. I was told they were varied in experience and publication. As I listened to them each give a brief introduction of who they were and what they write, I found that description to be true. And yet all were working on their craft. Some shared about new websites, articles published, or manuscripts waiting on a publisher's desk somewhere. There was a sense of pride and camaraderie as we celebrated and encouraged one another.

As I drove to the meeting I recognized this was part of the experiment. Writing is a part of me that I want to flourish during this crazy schedule I hold. I want to make time for it. And I have to. It won't happen on its own.

At the meeting, I was encouraged. As I listened to the discussion around the room—the questions, thoughts, and prayers—it was like listening to conversations in my own head. The fears, doubts, desires articulated were a mirror into my own creative space. And it reminded me this writing process is a wacky one. More importantly, it reminded me I am not alone.

Perhaps when stuck with two good options another question to ask is, God, which choice will better propel me toward being the person I want to become? That you want me to become?

I write to be an encouragement to someone else. To normalize, reassure, and maybe even challenge the woman who is reading my words. As I sat in that meeting I remembered what it is to be on the receiving end of normalization, that I, too, sometimes need to know I am not alone in caring about what I do care about. That having some people around who understand the publishing process or the tension of grammar is a good thing for me too.

My passions need fanning, especially in seasons where they may be lying low because of other responsibilities. Other people are great fans.

DAY 17

It's the end of summer and I am leaving my girls every morning to go write. We've had a great break, a lot of lazy days of not doing much, and some great adventures. But not a whole lot of writing has been done by their mama. So the compromise now—okay, the reality that the deadline is looming—is they need to spend some hours at home with the eldest in charge for me to work on this writing of mine.

This gets back to the rub doesn't it? That I am modeling to these young women in the making what it looks like to prioritize talents. And yet to do that I must leave them for a while, which can feel as a mom like I am not fully present for them. This is part of the myth of modern motherhood, that a mother must be always accessible to her children, and I too often believe it. I certainly don't want to pass that myth on to my girls, that I am less of a mother if I somehow dedicate a part of myself to something other than my children.

I balance the belief that God has made me for both mothering and whatever that passion might be, with the "do what only you can do" decision-making grid. No one else (thank goodness) can be their mother. And yet no one else can write this book either. I am created to follow God's call to do both.

I am not a fan of the phase philosophy either. That this is just a phase or a season and there will be time for (fill in the blank) later.

Because the truth is, we don't know that there will be a later. I've had too many, just too many, people I know or know of who were my age, vibrant adults, whose lives ended suddenly. I do not know that there will be a season for writing when my kids are older. I don't know where I'll be or where they'll be in five or ten years. I can do my best to make plans, but truly, if I was made to do something I must figure out a way to do that something now, even if a little at a time.

> *If I was made to do something I must figure out a way to do that something now, even if a little at a time.*

What I do know is that God knows the working out better than I do. So I go back to him with the question, *Lord, what do you have for me today?* It speaks back to that month of adventure of trusting God for the journey.

DAY 19

I opened my inbox this morning and found this blog post by Carolyn Custis James as she speaks about the world's story:

> The jaw-dropping moment for me comes early, when God speaks these words, "Let us make human beings in our image, in our likeness" and commissions his image bearers, male and female, to rule the whole earth on his behalf. This is the point at which we all enter God's story, not as bit players, but in leading roles. God calls all humanity to enter the story as his representatives, speaking and acting on his behalf and advancing his kingdom on earth.
>
> I'll spend the rest of my life unpacking all that God is giving us here. Yet, if even a little of this sinks in, nothing will be the same when my feet hit the floor in the morning. Knowing I have a strategic role in God's story changes everything.[6]

This is not a time to be passive, but to take an active role in what is happening in the world. Because it's my job. My job description, whittled down to the bare bones, is to love God with my whole heart and love those around me. Jesus said it plain as day.[7] And I overcomplicate things. I have plans, dreams, strategies, and even experiments to make things better and right. But all my efforts are for nothing if I don't love.

DAY 21

It's registration day at school. I'm flipping through boxes looking for immunization records and birth certificates, not really sure why I need to show these again. Their birthdates certainly haven't changed since last year when we did this same exercise.

For the youngers it means teacher assignments. And Gracie, who is going to big-girl, full-day school, has the same kindergarten teacher Genevieve did. And the teacher asked if I might be a room mom for the year.

I always thought I'd be the room mom. And the PTA president, while we're at it. It fit the picture I had for the kind of mother I'd be—ultra present, involved, mobilizing other parents. I've done those things, I think, but it hasn't looked like what I, and sometimes I think others, have thought it would. In fact, I've been to a total of two PTA meetings in my seven-year career as a public school parent.

But going back to work, writing books, traveling, and having more babies have kept me from stepping up. Especially in a place where there have been capable, dedicated parents. So I go to school, pick up my kids, and go home to write some more. Do what only you can do. I've tried to support and listen and carpool with the few friends right around me who have needed that.

But here was a teacher, the kind of person this authority-pleasing girl likes to please the most, asking if I would consider this job in a year when my workload will be less and I'll have only one at home to tote in and out of the school building. And I had a glimmer of a "maybe" in me. Now, I know I *can* do the job. Send emails and organize teacher gifts and make sure someone brings a gluten-free option to the Valentine's Day party. I am able to do these things, but there are lots of things I am able to do that could fill up my schedule and crowd out what makes me thrive. The question I should be asking is, Is it God's best for me for this year?

I also know there are lots of jobs no one wants. As my pastor Steve says, some people have to do diaper duty, meaning very few people are passionate about cleaning up poop, but in a community it needs to get done. Mostly, I thought of Gracie. Would this help her in the transition if I was at school a little more often, lingering at pick-up a little longer to talk with other parents, in stronger communication with her teacher? If one of my yeses stems from helping my girls transition into the next phase, would this be one?

> *My job description, whittled down to the bare bones, is to love God with my whole heart and love those around me.*

Some may say all of this pondering over a small volunteer job at school is overthinking. And yet I've lived with the consequences of the little commitments adding up. I need to stop this madness. And that starts right here with these kinds of little choices.

DAY 25

I responded to the kindergarten teacher that, yes, I would be able to be on the team of class parents. But with some conditions. The fall was out for me. Give me winter. Give me spring. But my workload in fall wouldn't allow me to take on more. There. Not a yes, not a no, but a here's what will work for me option.

I've never had space in my schedule to dedicate any time to a child's classroom. But this recalibrating has opened up some time. And yes, I can do this. I want to do this. Just not exactly as I'd pictured years ago. You know, before I was living my actual life.

DAY 27

I was on the phone with some other writers and speakers, talking about an upcoming retreat we were attending. And many of us admitted that, when we think of doing "great things for God," we think big. We think bestsellers and viral posts and sellout crowds. But that is the exact opposite of the gospel, of God, who chose to come as a newborn, who sat at the tables of ordinary people sharing one dinner at a time. My purpose is my task right in front of me, no matter the size of the job or how impressive it sounds to other people.

That blog post I read the other day from Carolyn Custis James captured it well.

> My life has kingdom significance. My story is a subject in the bigger story God is weaving. What I do with my life, from cradle to grave and no matter how mundane and ordinary, carries kingdom significance, a point made repeatedly in the Bible where so-called "little" people operating behind the scenes regularly advance God's kingdom. . . . God calls every image bearer to take their part in advancing his kingdom wherever he stations them.[8]

DAY 28

I've thought and prayed about the New York City opportunity and it sounds wonderful. New York is a place I think I will always want to say yes to visit. This city girl can never get enough of the people and sounds all smooshed together. And then to be able to see Spencer cross the Brooklyn Bridge! It would feel like adventure and passion all rolled up into one trip.

But the home front call is stronger for that particular week. Kindergarten prep and fourth grade. Seventh grade readiness. I want to create a sense of peace rather than chaos the last few days before these girls make a transition to new places and new people. I want lunch food stocked in the fridge and clean first-day-of-school outfits laid out and backpacks packed with all those glorious new school supplies. But more importantly, I want to do the tucking in at bedtime and the waking up.

Some might see this "no" as limiting, as confining. But if my passion truly is these people right here in front of me, saying yes to their needs is not confining; it's freeing. Because I am living out of where I feel God is calling me. I can only respond to my actual life. My actual choices and circumstances and passions. And for that week it is to be home helping my girls get ready for a new school year.

What I Learned

We live in a culture of big. Big-box stores, a thousand on-demand cable stations, big dreams. But what if our big *is* found in the small?

What if we do each small thing with great passion because we can? Because we are here and we are able to and yet do it with the knowledge we can't change the world in a day. But we can leave our small, unique imprint on it.

I had three objectives this month: to work on my writing, to help my girls transition to school, and to help Derek as he finishes up closing on this property. Because they were specific, I had an easier time figuring out where I needed to be, to do what only I could do. These weren't life-changing goals on their own, but more and more I'm recognizing life to be a series of small decisions that push in a certain direction. One small decision after another. Like a string of lights, one small light at a time makes an impact.

> My purpose is my task right in front of me, no matter the size of the job or how impressive it sounds to other people.

And in a life where we are faced with conflicting good things, we are forced to make choices. I'm learning "do what only you can do" helps. So does prayer, considering God holds it all. He alone understands the clash of demands and desires in my schedule and heart. He made me for certain purposes with certain talents. It makes sense I would look to him to help me discern where to focus my attention today.

Practices I'll Continue

Determine what only I can do.

Write every week.

Ask my family what I can do for them.

Say no more often than I say yes.

Pray through decisions.

Questions for Reflection

1. Think of a time when you have had to make a choice between two good things. How did the process go? How did you ultimately make your decision?
2. Name what only you can do right now.
3. What decisions can you make to move toward becoming the person you want? The person God wants?

Words for My Actual Life

So, no matter what I say, what I believe, and what I do, I'm bankrupt without love. (1 Cor. 13:3 Message)

Conclusion

THIS ONE LIFE

Lying in bed, I could see only sky out the window, the clouds a bright pink. It was sunrise and I could feel the snugglers, those who snuck into our bed in the middle of the night, still sleeping next to me. I closed my eyes for not more than a minute and opened them again to see the clouds had changed. As the sun was moving higher into the sky on the other side of the house, the pink reflection in the clouds was swirling and moving. Had I not opened my eyes again, I would have missed that moment. And the next. And the next.

One life. Portioned into segments. Years. Months. Weeks. Days. Hours. Minutes. Seconds.

One life God has granted for now. It is temporary. It is now. And if I'm not careful I might miss it.

One life unique to me. Not like anyone else's, nor should it be, and yet I'm always longing for that next thing.

One life I want to cherish. I want to hold close and appreciate. To not waste. To not take for granted.

Do I know any better today how to fully relish this actual life than I did nine months ago? Did this experiment do anything in helping me love the now? Looking back, I developed some practices and gained some insights while in experiment mode that helped me view my life through a new lens.

Noticing

When something is at the forefront of your mind you begin to notice it in unexpected places. Each month as I've considered, wondered, tried, failed, and tried again to capture something new about a particular area of my life, I've simply noticed that area and its influence on me more. Quiet. Creativity. My body. Because it's been the designated focus of my attention, I've noticed what's right in front of me.

> *Do I know any better today how to fully relish this actual life than I did nine months ago?*

The way I feel with no dinner plan compared to when there is one.

The free hour at soccer practice that can be spent with those sitting next to me.

The relaxed feeling I have when I walk into a room and it's somewhat orderly.

This act of noticing has not only helped prompt me toward change but has made me grateful for where I am and what I have. Because not only am I considering what I'm striving for, I'm recognizing what is already here.

Acting

Not as in playacting, pretending, but as in taking action. This experiment pushed me to not just talk about an area, but actually try something new to see if it helped me love this life a little more. Often that meant doing the thing I didn't want to. What's been heightened in all my noticing is that I'm a procrastinator. Worse, I'm an avoider. I avoid dealing with certain tasks that overwhelm me (home organization is the number one example). And I could let that could go on forever.

The experiment pushed me to address some areas of avoidance for me. I couldn't just add them to the end of the to-do list where they are often placed, but moved them to the top. (Exercise, anyone?) And when I really jumped in and dealt with that thing that was hanging over my head, whatever it was, I felt a burden lifted on the other side. And usually the act of dealing with the issue itself was not as bad as I'd anticipated. In other words, I was more stressed avoiding the task than actually doing it.

The rewards of taking charge seemed to be compounded. Every time I stood in my cleaned closet I felt myself relax a little. Every time I knew what was for dinner—or better yet, lunch—I could breathe. When I looked in the mirror as I ran by it on my way out the door to school drop-offs in the morning and saw a relatively well-dressed woman, I felt ready to face the day. So jumping from "I wish this was different" to actually making it different had a noticeable impact. And the more success I had, the more motivated I was to take on the next little change and the next.

Scheduling

It turns out the schedule rules. If I put something on my schedule it is more likely to happen. This is not revolutionary, I realize. But it is a discipline. To recognize exercise or time with someone is truly a priority means I will make time on my schedule to give it what it deserves. This of course impacts items on my calendar that go on without much thought. If my life is at capacity, I must cut something to add something else. Reserving that hour or evening ahead of time ensures I will get to that thing I truly value.

Failing

As a mom I hear myself say pithy things like, "You can't succeed unless you fail," or "Trying and failing is how you learn," all the time. No wonder my children roll their eyes at me (yes, even the now-four-year-old). Cliché words don't stick. But like many mom-isms, they are based in truth.

I have found through the experiment the things that work for me. For my actual life with my actual family and my actual personality. Often I've learned what *does* work by discovering what doesn't. Likely you read some of my experiments and thought, *Who is she kidding? Dumbest idea ev-ah*. Or *Really? Why didn't that work for her? I can do that in my sleep.*

I truly did think buying some type of organizational chart would help my house get organized. And I believed wearing my yoga pants would encourage me to exercise. It turns out these things are not true for me. All they did was add to the guilt that I wasn't getting more done. But in the fails I learned some things about how I operate, what is realistic in my life today with my circumstances.

Failure is not the focus here; success is. All those lessons about what won't work for me point toward what *will*. What *will* offer me more quiet. What *will* allow me to have quality one-on-one time with the people I love most. What *will* help spur some creativity in my life. So I'm grateful for that learning along the way.

The Power of Small

These little, minor changes made a difference in my everyday. They truly did. Could I do all of them all of the time? No, I would drive myself crazy. But could I figure out a few things that make me feel a little better about my day? Certainly. The sink is full of dishes and has been for two days. I now know how much better I'll feel when I pass through my kitchen (about two million times per day) if I address that issue. Do I feel disconnected from my eldest? I know sending her a text right in that moment will allow me to communicate I'm thinking about her.

As I wipe down the inside of the fridge, I remind myself this will be a gift in an hour when I open it again. I close my computer and listen to my girl share about her day. I tell myself this parenting thing is cumulative and I am adding one more drop of message that she matters to me into her being. I light a candle and notice the ambiance in the room change immediately. It's every little bulb on a string that together make a string of lights. As Meghan says, life is big in the little.

My actual life is evidence of that. The big can be seen and experienced in the little. No better example than Jesus, God of the universe, who came to this earth as a baby. A tiny human baby. He who has the whole world in his hands came in the tiniest human form we can conceive.

Yes, life is big in the little, and I can say I'm more aware of it now than I was nine months ago. And I'm taking my lessons with me. All of that noticing. I've tucked into my mind what works and I'm putting into place with more intentionality and awareness what is right in front of me and what I'm doing about it.

God's Covering Is Everywhere

All this noticing pointed toward one larger truth: God's presence in the details. Does he care what I'm eating or wearing or cleaning? Does he care where I am putting my attention? If it impacts my ability to follow his commandments to love him and love others then I think he does. When he was walking around this planet, Jesus was pretty clear with people that behavior mattered because behavior showed the state of the heart. In these terms I think Jesus cares about how we live because he cares about the state of our hearts.

The covering is everywhere because I can see his miracles everywhere. In the people I interact with, in how my body works, in the trees on my street, and in my children's tears. It all points to a Creator who paid attention to the details when he created us, and all this noticing helps me recognize these gifts and relish them while they are here.

His covering of grace is also unavoidable. When I failed at an experiment, did God love me any less? No. His character, his essence, does not change. I can't move his position toward me. So in a sense those failures not only taught me about my own wiring, they reminded me of what I already knew of his, that his grace covers every area of my life. I, in fact, do not need to perform for him.

This One Life Matters

I'm not a superstar, except maybe to a few people on this planet. But what more could I want? Really? To influence a tiny group in seriously meaningful ways.

For some of Derek's coworkers at Providence Network, those they live with in a Prov home are their self-determined family circle, their tight group. For others it may be an organized group from their church or an informal group of friends who are their people. Regardless of who that group is for you, you matter to them. Your words, attention, interests matter. Invest your relishing, your noticing, right where you are, and God will use it for his purposes.

Because this is the place where our lives and God's purposes intersect. This one life we've been given. How will we use it today? It doesn't have to be with thousands of "followers"; it has to be right here in our core. With our Creator hearing our prayers, knowing our heart churnings, feeling our feelings right along with us. It is here in our innermost places that we relish that we are made as image bearers and we live out of that creative genius.

It is here that we make our mark on the world—one conversation, one help, one prayer at a time.

There is no show here. Just an earnest desire to be my best and live my best so God will say I used this one life well.

Loving My Actual Life

Loving. Really loving it? I think I do. And yet there are a million distractions from the goodness. The whole point of these last nine months, I suppose.

My life. Not her life. Or your life. But mine. Circumstances and details that have been assigned to me by chance, by choice on my part or others', by God's design. Sometimes it's difficult to distinguish between those, but it really doesn't matter. It's the only life I have and I'm the only one who can claim it as my own. It's a coming to terms with and embracing.

Actual. Not virtual. Not imagined. Not dreamed of. The circumstances or details are not as I would wish or design if I were in charge. But that's part of the exercise, right? The loving within what is, rather than what I wish would be. So I look at them honestly, these parts that make up my every day, and I am grateful for the good. And I even work to be grateful for the difficult because I know, though painful, it can shape me for the better. So in all things I give thanks.

Life. That breathing, pulsing, beating portion of time that I am here. Because I guess that is what defines a life in part, the time you are here and what happens in it. And Jesus who says he is "the life"[1] beckons me to come to him for more. Because just as he says he is the life, he says, "Come." *All you tired, overwhelmed people, come and I will give you rest.*[2] So yes, I want to love these days, hours, minutes I have here and I want to draw closer to the One who breathes life in. Because I want to know I've done my best with this one life when I pass from it to the next.

So did this experiment make a difference? I say yes. Because these nine months pushed me closer to noticing the moments, to gratitude, and to an awareness of God's presence. Toward understanding the life I want and the person I want to become.

Toward loving my actual life.

Questions for Reflection

1. How does noticing impact your ability to relish what's right in front of you?
2. How do actions change your immediate quality of life?
3. Where do you see God's covering?

Words for My Actual Life

I have learned to be content whatever the circumstances. I know what it is to be in need, and I know what it is to have plenty. I have learned the secret of being content in any and every situation, whether well fed or hungry, whether living in plenty or in want. I can do all this through him who gives me strength. (Phil. 4:11–13)

Ideas to Love Your Actual Life

TEN THINGS TO TRY WHEN DESIGNING YOUR OWN EXPERIMENT

Needing some ideas for your own experiment? Consider this a menu of possibilities, not a prescription for success. Do none. Do some. Do them all. Remember, this is about *you* loving *your* actual life, so choose ideas that will help you make needed tweaks in each of these areas.

Quiet

1. Have a designated thirty minutes of quiet.
2. Practice breath prayer.
3. Take a social media break.
4. Get up before or go to bed after everyone else in your home.
5. Take a walk alone.
6. Turn off music, phones, and passengers' movies when driving.
7. Read a passage of Scripture.

8. Take a technology fast (computers, television, i-anything).
9. Designate a day of the week to be your day off or "Sabbath."
10. Enjoy being in others' company without conversation.

Mornings

1. Make breakfast and/or lunches the night before.
2. Create a prioritized daily to-do list.
3. Get up first for some quiet, prayer, and a warm drink.
4. Get dressed with the idea of presenting your best self to the day (have a fallback uniform).
5. Make your bed.
6. Tidy up (especially the kitchen) before leaving the house.
7. Lay out everyone's clothes the night before.
8. Have a morning routine checklist for every member of your family.
9. Create a staging area for leaving the house.
10. Change plans when needed.

Dates

1. Schedule specific dates with specific people and put them on your calendar.
2. When tempted to browse on your phone, call a friend instead.
3. Ask the person next to you open-ended questions.
4. Discover the "love languages" of those around you.
5. Put a movie on for the kids and have an at-home date with your spouse.
6. Play a game as a family after dinner.
7. Take a child with you on an errand or to a sibling's game/ practice.

8. Invite someone over for dinner. Tonight!
9. Attend a worship service.
10. Have a designated spot for everyone to turn in phones when arriving home.

Health

1. Make a list of all the things your body allows you to do.
2. Exercise three times this week.
3. Schedule doctor/dentist appointments for yourself.
4. Go to bed an hour earlier than usual.
5. Play an active game with your kids.
6. Set a designated screen end time for the day.
7. Invest in good shoes and clothes for exercise.
8. Replace soda or coffee with water.
9. Say a prayer of gratitude for your body.
10. Take a nap.

Adventure

1. Stay in a hotel in your hometown.
2. Create a meal around a new ingredient.
3. Drive home by a different route.
4. Sign up for a class to learn something new (or watch a video online).
5. Support someone else's adventure.
6. Rearrange the furniture in a room.
7. Take public transportation to a new neighborhood.
8. Visit a new park or trail.
9. Dress up for dinner (fancy or theme related).
10. Go "treasure hunting" in garage sales.

Home Organization

1. Set a decorating/organizing goal and invite someone over to see the end result.
2. Pick up items to put away as you walk through a room.
3. Have two designated clean-up times a day.
4. Set a timer as you clean, then say "good enough."
5. Organize one closet or cupboard.
6. Touch everything once.
7. Change out the pictures in frames.
8. Have an area ready and available for an unexpected guest.
9. Paint one wall.
10. Pray for your home to be a refuge for all who visit and live there.

Creativity

1. Take a walk or hike.
2. Read/write a poem.
3. Listen to a full song with your eyes closed.
4. Color in a coloring book.
5. Buy yourself fresh flowers.
6. Play classical music in your house.
7. Make something with tools.
8. Try a new recipe.
9. Plant in a pot or garden.
10. Use found items to decorate a spot in your house.

Meals

1. Develop a list of staples to keep stocked in your pantry.
2. Double what you make and freeze it.

3. Know what you are having for dinner by 10:00 a.m. each day.
4. Invite someone, or a whole group, over for breakfast.
5. Say a prayer of gratitude before every meal or snack.
6. Make a meal plan for five days in a row.
7. Choose one person to celebrate and make a meal in their honor.
8. Eat outside or have a picnic on the floor.
9. Put on music, light candles, or have a special drink while making dinner.
10. Involve your family in meal planning and prep.

Passions

1. Do an activity you loved as a child.
2. Read an article on something you are interested in.
3. Make a list of your unique skills and talents.
4. Decide what "Do what only you can do" means for you today.
5. Take an assessment like StrengthsFinder to learn about yourself.
6. Say yes to something and no to something else.
7. Set a timer for thirty minutes and do one small thing that will feed into your area of passion.
8. Learn to do one thing really well (a recipe, a technique).
9. Listen to a podcast on a topic of interest.
10. Make a choice between two good things.

Acknowledgments

A book is truly a team effort. (Especially when the author is trying to still get food on the table. You know, the whole actual life thing.)

Thank you to the team of professionals and readers who helped this book writing happen. To Bill Jensen for believing in me and Teresa Evenson for representing and encouraging me throughout this process. To Rebekah Guzman and the team at Baker Books for signing on to publish this experiment. To Carla Foote and Nicci Jordan Hubert for your editing skills; you made my words count while you counted my words. To Annie, Lindsey, Erica, Jean, and Carol for reading the earliest versions of chapters. Thank you all.

And to my everyday, every day people who made this happen, thank you. The ones in the book and the ones on the sidelines, you are my actual people, my actual life. To my extended family for helping with the practical so I could think for more than twenty seconds at a time (the grandmothers get a special shout-out here); I couldn't have done it without you. And to my main cast of characters, thank you for letting me write during soccer practice and summer mornings and everywhere in between to squeeze this book out in the middle of our "crazy busy" life.

To those who make appearances in these pages, I understand doing life with me has its quirks. Thank you for letting me share in a public way so others might see normal in their own stories.

And to the greatest author and storyteller, the Father, Son, and Holy Ghost, I do not understand why you extended such grace when you gave me this one life. May I never take it for granted, but use it for your purposes and your glory. Thank you for my actual life.

Notes

Introduction

1. Matthew 11:28.
2. Ephesians 2:8 Message.
3. Mothers of Preschoolers, www.MOPS.org.

Month 1

1. "Noisy Surroundings Take Toll on Short Term Memory," Max Planck Society, September 7, 2012, http://www.mpg.de/6342752/acoustics_short-term-memory.
2. "Cell Phone Call May Spur Blood Pressure Spike," *HuffPost Healthy Living*, May 17, 2013, http://www.huffingtonpost.com/2013/05/17/cell-phone-blood-pressure-_n_3294462.html.
3. "Mindfulness," Anderson Cooper, *60 Minutes*, December 14, 2014, http://www.cbsnews.com/news/mindfulness-anderson-cooper-60-minutes.
4. Adele Ahlberg Calhoun, *Spiritual Disciplines Handbook: Practices That Transform Us* (InterVarsity Press, 2005), 205.
5. Ibid.
6. John Ortberg, *Soul Keeping: Caring for the Most Important Part of You* (Grand Rapids: Zondervan, 2014), 140.
7. Luke 2:25–35.
8. Calhoun, *Spiritual Disciplines Handbook*, 86.
9. Matthew 14:22–23.
10. Mother Teresa, BrainyQuote.com, http://www.brainyquote.com/quotes/quotes/m/mothertere164357.html.

Month 2

1. Psalm 37:7.
2. Matthew 11:28.
3. Kathi Lipp, *Clutter Free: Quick and Easy Steps to Simplifying Your Space* (Eugene, OR: Harvest House Publishers, 2015), 89.

Month 3

1. "Jim Gaffigan: Mr. Universe—4 KIDS," YouTube, October 9, 2012, https://www.youtube.com/watch?t=3&v=GEbZrY0G9PI.
2. Sarah Pulliam Bailey, "Want 'Sustained Happiness'? Get Religion, Study Suggests," *The Washington Post*, August 14, 2015, http://www.washingtonpost.com/news/acts-of-faith/wp/2015/08/14/want-sustained-happiness-get-religion-study-suggests.
3. Tara M. Owens, *Embracing the Body: Finding God in Our Flesh and Bone* (InterVarsity Press 2015), 230.
4. Pope Francis, BrainyQuote.com, http://www.brainyquote.com/quotes/quotes/p/popefranci571222.html.
5. James 4:8.
6. Gary Chapman and Ross Campbell, *The 5 Love Languages of Children* (Chicago: Northfield Publishing, 2005), 25.

Month 4

1. Krissy Brady, "Why Are Modern Women So Exhausted?," *Women's Health*, October 21, 2013, http://www.womenshealthmag.com/health/exhaustion?page=2.
2. World Water Day, http://www.unwater.org/worldwaterday/learn/en.
3. Carolyn Mahaney and Nicole Whitacre, *True Beauty* (Chicago: Crossway, 2014), 56.
4. Owens, *Embracing the Body*, 176.

Month 5

1. Stasi Eldredge, April 2, 2015, https://www.facebook.com/StasiEldredge/posts/676815945797916.
2. Jennie Allen, *Chase Study Guide: Chasing After the Heart of God* (Nashville: Thomas Nelson, 2012), 18.
3. Jesse Paul, Kieran Nicholson, and Carlos Illescas, "Two Guns Seized, 3 Boys Arrested at Denver Middle School; No Injuries," *The Denver Post*, April 10, 2015, http://www.denverpost.com/news/ci_27887086/denver-police-skinner-middle-school-locked-down-weapon.
4. Psalm 23:1–4.
5. Alina Tugend, "Tiptoeing Out of One's Comfort Zone (and Of Course, Back In)," *New York Times*, February 11, 2011, http://www.nytimes.com/2011/02/12/your-money/12shortcuts.html?pagewanted=all&_r=1.

Month 6

1. Yolanda Williams, "Environmental Stressors: Examples, Definitions & Types," http://study.com/academy/lesson/environmental-stressors-examples -definition-types.html.

2. William H. McRaven, quoted in Peter Jacobs, "Navy SEAL Commander Tells Students to Make Their Beds Every Morning in Incredible Commencement Speech," May 20, 2014, http://www.businessinsider.com/bill-mcraven-commence ment-speech-at-ut-2014-5.

3. Ibid.

4. Greg McKeown, *Essentialism: The Disciplined Pursuit of Less* (New York: Crown Publishing Group, 2014), 17.

5. Matthew 25:35–36.

Month 7

1. Amanda Enayati, "A Creative Life Is a Healthy Life," CNN, May 26, 2012, http://www.cnn.com/2012/05/25/health/enayati-innovation-passion-stress.

2. Emily P. Freeman, *A Million Little Ways: Uncover the Art You Were Made to Live* (Grand Rapids: Revell, 2013), 22–23.

3. Jim Gaffigan, "King Baby—Camping," YouTube, October 27, 2010, https:// www.youtube.com/watch?v=ZdqIpYhM6PE.

4. http://www.sixwordmemoirs.com.

5. Laura Vanderkam, *168 Hours: You Have More Time Than You Think* (New York: Penguin Books, 2010), 183–84.

6. Matthew 10:30.

7. Psalm 8:1–9 Message.

8. Shawn Anchor, "Are the People Who Take Vacations the Ones Who Get Promoted?," *Harvard Business Review*, June 12, 2015, https://hbr.org/2015/06/are -the-people-who-take-vacations-the-ones-who-get-promoted.

Month 8

1. Karen S. Hamerick, Margaret Andrews, Joanne Guthrie, David Hopkins, and Ket McClelland, "How Much Time Do Americans Spend on Food?," USDA ERS, Economic Information Bulletin Number 86, November 2011, http://www .ers.usda.gov/media/149404/eib86.pdf.

2. A. Coleman-Jensen, M. Rabbitt, C. Gregory, and A. Singh, "Household Food Security in the United States in 2014," USDA ERS, 2015, http://www.feeding america.org/hunger-in-america/impact-of-hunger/child-hunger/child-hunger -fact-sheet.html.

3. Krista Gilbert, *Reclaiming Home: A Family's Guide for Life, Love & Legacy* (New York: Morgan James Publishing, 2015), 119.

4. Matthew 6:11.

5. Genesis 1:29–31 Message.

6. Genesis 2:1–2 Message.

7. Matthew 14:13–21.

8. Matthew 4:4 Message.

9. http://www.colorado-demographics.com/walsenburg-demographics.

Month 9

1. Dave Kerpen, "15 Inspiring Quotes on Passion (Get Back to What You Love)," *Inc.com*, http://www.inc.com/dave-kerpen/15-quotes-on-passion-to-inspire-a-better-life.html.

2. See MOPS International 2013–14 group video curriculum.

3. 1 Corinthians 13:1–7 Message.

4. Ruth Chang, "How to Make Hard Choices," TED.com, June 2014, http://www.ted.com/talks/ruth_chang_how_to_make_hard_choices/transcript?language=en.

5. Ibid.

6. Carolyn Custis James, "Your Place in the Story," *Really* (blog), August 4, 2015, http://www.elisamorgan.com/#!Your-Place-in-the-Story/cnmy/55bffd9a0cf267673a81e8cd.

7. Luke 10:27.

8. James, "Your Place in the Story."

Conclusion

1. John 14:6.

2. Matthew 11:28.

Alexandra Kuykendall spends most of her days driving to and from different schools and searching for a better solution to the laundry dilemma. On staff with MOPS International for nearly ten years, Alex is a trusted voice in mothering circles. Her writings include *The Artist's Daughter: A Memoir*, chronicling her journey from childhood to motherhood. A city girl at heart, she lives in the shadows of downtown Denver with her husband and their four daughters. You can connect with her at AlexandraKuykendall.com.

CONNECT WITH

Alex

ALEXANDRAKUYKENDALL.COM

@Alex_Kuykendall

AlexandraKuykendall.Author

Alexandra Kuykendall

LOVE this book?

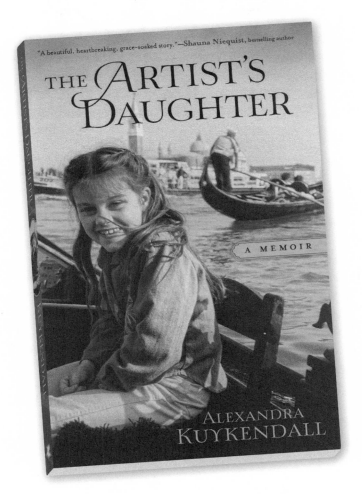

ALSO AVAILABLE BY

Alexandra Kuykendall

LIKE THIS
BOOK?
Consider sharing
it with others!

- Share or mention the book on your social media platforms. Use the hashtag #LovingMyActualLife.

- Write a book review on your blog or on a retailer site.

- Pick up a copy for friends, family, or strangers! Anyone who you think would enjoy and be challenged by its message.

- Share this message on Twitter or Facebook: **"Read #LovingMyActualLife by @Alex_Kuykendall // @ReadBakerBooks"**

- Recommend this book for your church, workplace, book club, or class.

- Follow Baker Books on social media and tell us what you like.

 Facebook.com/ReadBakerBooks

 @ReadBakerBooks

with all of its ups and downs, joys and challenges, Alexandra Kuykendall convincingly reminds me to embrace and cherish what I have. Her nine-month experiment touches on the topics and areas that are accessible and relatable to every woman who is juggling work-life-family and striving to flourish in the fullness of her vocational calling. Reading this book is like the gift of deeply connecting with a dear friend, one who will not judge me because she gets me. My challenges are her challenges, and she lives them every day. Yet she is filled with immense hope and knowledge that neither of us is stuck. With practical and insightful tips, tools, and lessons learned, along with some experimentation, she encourages me along the journey of living fully and loving my actual life."

Cindy Chang Mahlberg, cofounder, Women in the Mix;
chief exploration officer, The Law Venture

"As moms we can't help but compare: ourselves, our homes, our kids. Yet as we do we miss our actual life. We allow our unrealistic ideals to darken our days. Enough! Within these pages Alex shares her heart—and her journey—to prioritize her life. She shares her goals, her struggles, and lessons learned. Alex shows us that life isn't about a point to be reached but rather ways to make the most of the life you already have. Wonderful!"

Tricia Goyer, author of *Balanced: Finding Center
as a Work-at-Home Mom*

"There is a constant tension between the way we imagined life would be and the way life actually *is*. We find ourselves continually wanting more, but we just aren't sure where or how to get it. In her signature poignant, clever, insightful, and nonjudgmental writing style, Alexandra Kuykendall helps us see that the 'more' we desire is not only within our grasp but right in front of us. Rarely is there a book where practical tips intersect with personal story in such an engaging, interesting, and life-changing way. What I may love the most about *Loving My Actual Life*, however, is that Alexandra lives what she writes. Out of her real-life experiences and authenticity comes a guide to help us trade the illusion of a perfect life for one that holds 'more.' More depth, more love, and more joy."

Krista Gilbert, author of *Reclaiming Home*; blogger at kristagilbert.com

"Along with her daughters in *Loving My Actual Life*, I raise a champagne flute of chocolate milk to Alex for taking us along on her experiment of living intentionally. She shows us it's possible to embrace our real lives and enjoy the moments along the way. We have one life and this book calls us to love it, even in the mundane, messes, and meal planning. Read it! You'll love the book. Come to find out, you might love your actual life."

Sarah Harmeyer, founder and chief people gatherer, Neighbor's Table

"If you ever get the chance to read anything written by Alexandra Kuyken-dall, take it. She is a gentle, trustworthy storyteller who lives the words she writes. In a noisy world, I deeply appreciate her thoughtful, grounded voice."

Emily P. Freeman, author of *Simply Tuesday*

"We can spend our lives wishing for tomorrow or decide to enjoy God's goodness today. In *Loving My Actual Life*, Alex shares how we can cherish each season and find the gold already there. Grab a friend, or ten, to share in this experiment to love *your* actual life."

Rebekah Lyons, author of *Freefall to Fly*

"Most of us struggle to like our lives, let alone love them. We look around and want what *she* has or to be like *her*. And so we miss *our* lives—our actual lives. There are lots of books about home organization, self-improvement, and workout routines. This book is different. Starting off with a call to quiet, Alexandra Kuykendall dares herself to invest intentionally in her daily life and discovers not just how to survive but how to love her life. *Loving My Actual Life* is entertaining and insightful, honest and winsome, challenging and comforting. Here is the journal of a woman who found contentment by choosing it and shares with us how we can as well."

Elisa Morgan, speaker; author of *The Beauty of Broken* and *Hello, Beauty Full*; cohost, *Discover the Word* radio show; president emerita, MOPS International

"In this book Alex does what I think most of us secretly wish we could—she makes time and space for that list of things we all have, the things we want to do but never have time for. Over nine months she deliberately changes her life so that it starts to work for her, instead of her maniacally trying to work to keep up with her life. Hands up if you can relate? If you're tired of putting off all those things you keep wanting to do differently in your family, Alex will be the friend who keeps you company when you decide to start. Preferably tomorrow."

Lisa-Jo Baker, author of *Surprised by Motherhood*; community manager for (in)courage

"Alexandra Kuykendall's heart shines brightly in this gently written ex-periment of discovering God's gifts in the midst of the grind. Alex doesn't gloss over the painful realities and hardships of our daily lives. Rather, she invites us to savor the goodness that is right in front of us—the goodness that we are prone to miss when we're always longing for how life should be rather than appreciating what actually is."

Jeannie Cunnion, author of *Parenting the Wholehearted Child*

"How many times have I looked at other people's lives and wished for some aspect of what they have? By providing us a window into her own life